GROUP WORK WITH OVERWHELMED CLIENTS

How the Power of Groups Can
Help People Transform
Their Lives

JUNE GARY HOPPS
ELAINE PINDERHUGHES

THE FREE PRESS

The Free Press
A Division of Simon & Schuster
1230 Avenue of the Americas
New York, NY 10020

The Free Press and colophon are trademarks
of Simon & Schuster Inc.

Designed by Carla Bolte

Manufactured in the United States of America
10 9 8 7 6 5 4 3 2 1

Library of Congress Cataloging-In-Publication Data

Hopps, June G.
        Group work with overwhelmed clients : how the power of groups can
help people transform their lives / June Gary Hopps, Elaine
Pinderhughes.
        p. cm.
    Includes bibliographical references and index.
    ISBN: 0-7432-3786-2
    1. Group psychotherapy.   2. Social group work.   3. Group
counseling.   I. Pinderhughes, Elaine.   II. Title.
RC488.H65   1999
616.89'152—dc21   98-34825
                                           CIP

For information regarding special discounts for bulk purchases, please contact Simon &
Schuster Special Sales at 1-800-456-6798 or business@simonandschuster.com

To

JOHN HOPPS

and

CHARLES PINDERHUGHES

CONTENTS

ACKNOWLEDGMENTS

To Anna Faith Jones and the Boston Foundation, we offer sincere thanks for their support of this project.

We are also appreciative of the assistance we received from many practitioners who shared their first-hand knowledge about groups with us. These dedicated professionals came from a number of disciplines: clinical social work, psychology, law enforcement, sociology, and theology. Without their contribution, this book could not have been written. We thank immensely: Sonia Pinnock, Marque Fraizer, Ken Hardy, Lani Jones, Debbie Lynn, Majorie Schwartz Thomsen, Hugo Kamya, Tom Walsh, Carl Taylor, Howard Pinderhughes, Matthew Hopps, Anne Freed, and Theodore Howe.

We also express our gratitude to Free Press editors Susan Arellano, for suggesting this book and shepherding it through the early process, and Philip Rappaport, for seeing it to completion; and to our Boston College colleagues, Mary Hogan, Evelyn Aleman-Zuniga, and Josephine Connors for their administrative support.

GROUP WORK WITH OVERWHELMED CLIENTS

1

A MANDATE FOR GROUPS

In *The Power to Care,*[1] a study on clinical effectiveness, we described empirically based findings that demonstrate success in helping clients who are overwhelmed by personal, socioeconomic, and environmental problems to move to higher levels of functioning. Our findings highlighted promising interventions and underscored the significance for clinicians of helping skills that are anchored in flexible functioning, in respect for and understanding of their clients' culture, and in the capacity to hold them to high expectations.

Interventions that hold promise include effective assessment, advocacy, empowerment, individual treatment, and group treatment. Group treatment was actually highly effective, with particularly dramatic outcomes in work with youthful populations, but surprisingly it was not the intervention of choice. Why was this so? Pursuing answers to this seemingly simple question has challenged us to further thought and investigation, with the goal of identifying the philosophical, institutional/operational, professional, and/or practitioner barriers that block or retard the use of groups as an interventive modality. Paradoxically, while groups were not widely used in clinical work with clients, they were used for training, and for sustaining and supporting staff in their work with clients. Despite the fact that groups were used to empower staff, there was little evidence that this resource and knowledge was applied to clients and their communities as a means of empowerment. We question whether or not a conceptual connection has been overlooked between the needs for staff development and growth and community needs for growth and development.

In seeking to understand the connection between the use of groups and the successful outcomes achieved in work with overwhelmed clients we noted several factors: the impact of group participation on the functioning of these clients, the bonding between members, the validation and support derived from members, as well as the role model of the professional group facilitator. To explore these aspects of group process and success in work with this population we pondered the following: What roles do group leaders play, both professionally and nonprofessionally? What do they bring to the various stages of group formation, development, and termination? Given the importance and need for models in the lives of clients, what, if any, attributes, skills, and/or values do clients learn from leaders or facilitators? Some of the group experiences brought support to members as they were struggling with pressing problems that earlier generations had never faced. These included groups for children whose parents were infected with HIV/AIDS, support groups for college women and new immigrant women, therapeutic groups, mixed gender groups, groups for troubled gang youths, for parents who were drug addicts in recovery, and for women dealing with sexual and domestic abuse often precipitated by drug or alcohol addiction. In observing the way drugs have taken over far too many lives, wrecking marriages or relationships, destroying families and communities, we pondered the response of agencies to this phenomenon and the role of groups in helping people manage the consequences of addiction and learn to manage their lives free from drugs. Some examples are presented in the several chapters that follow.

We became deeply concerned about the vulnerability of children under these conditions, and in particular their vulnerability to relational starvation. What about the child whose parents are addicts and whose grandparent, unable to cope, is forced to give up that grandchild to a flawed foster care system? Can there be a promising future for that child? Multiply this scenario—block by block, neighborhood by neighborhood. What you have are a number of fragmented and disconnected families and neighborhoods that create individuals who have not learned to care for or about one another. Sucked as they are into the commodity identity so idealized today, they become obsessed with acquiring the material goods which they believe can add meaning to their empty lives. For example, even while she was in a recovery group, one addicted mother was preoccupied with how she could obtain the expensive clothing, toys, jewelry, and electronic equipment for her children that her drug pushing and using boyfriend had been providing. She worried:

> What will my kids think when they can't get new clothes every week? What will my kids say when their friends talk about them and how they look in old stuff?

From our research it has seemed logical to conclude that unless new national policy initiatives provide opportunities for work at decent wages and pro-family services such as basic health care, and unless these are complemented by nurturing and supportive neighborhood-level family services, effective educational programs, day care, and child development activities, there will be an escalation in the circular reinforcing problems that are symptomatic of client entrapment and powerlessness: poverty, drug and alcohol addiction, gangs and undisciplined children, domestic violence, sexual abuse, mental disorders, and community-wide destructiveness.

Our findings suggest that there may be emerging a stronger role and place for professionally led groups in contemporary society as a moderating and hopeful force for addressing both personal and societal problems. Such groups can provide a much-needed sense of connection to others for those suffering from abandonment and a sense of alienation due to societal conditions.

We think groups represent a powerful and underutilized resource for the helping professions to assist clients in repairing the disconnection and relationship starvation from which many suffer, providing the supports necessary for survival, empowerment, personal growth, and change. Groups can also address the need for neighborhood empowerment and growth, thereby effecting change on both individual and societal levels.

HIGH EXPECTATIONS

Another finding from *The Power to Care*—that effective outcome is associated with practitioners who have high expectations for their clients—may have far-reaching heuristic value. This finding concerning practitioners' tendencies to hold clients to a high standard of functioning, to believe in their capacity to cope successfully, may be inconsistent with the traditional helping approach that focuses on "the problem," dysfunction, and pathology. Holding high expectations means focusing on strengths and requires practitioners to be very comfortable with the goal of client empowerment. A clinician who focuses on strength and is able to use her own power to empower her client must be flexible, able to identify, support, and enhance strengths, and must eschew a focus on pathology and on the use of labels in ways that reinforce pathology. Practitioners who have a personal need to be the expert and the powerful one may not be able to focus on strengths and may be unable to push the client to action that will lead to greater competence or equal power in the relationship. As the reader will see in a case described later on, one practitioner who worked with a mothers' group demonstrated this capacity in her expectations of one of the group's members.

EMPOWERMENT AND POWERLESS SOCIETAL ROLES

In the course of our research for the book we noted how difficult it is for practitioners to sustain a diverse group when certain constellations related to powerless societal roles exist. Staff who recruited white and Latino women for one mothers' group were not successful in sustaining the interest of many. Why? We proffer ideas about the role of the practitioner and the dynamics of power and powerlessness related to race, gender, and social class, and then develop a conceptual framework that we believe will guide work in this area. We acknowledge that all of these variables are significant in clients' problems, clinical process, and outcomes in this work. Each of these dimensions of social status represents a significant influence in the relationship of practitioner and group and of group member to group member. Although all members of a given group may be people of color and poor, their experience of poverty and oppression stemming from ethnic identity and national origin and their perception of obstacles to be overcome will be different. Thus while the group's members will exhibit some similarities, there are also differences which must be appreciated, respected, and ultimately negotiated. These dynamics compound the complexities embodied in work with this population.

WHY GROUPS CAN BE DIFFICULT TO START

Group activities are often hard to deliver in the face of certain day-to-day logistical realities. First, there are the dynamics of getting started; often people must languish on a waiting list until enough persons with the appropriate characteristics are available to start a group. Second, group attendance can be compromised by participants' anxieties related to threatening outside activities. For example, a parent may be anxious about what day and at what time a particular drug activity is to take place and what will happen if law enforcement tries to pull a bust. Third, and especially during evenings, there may be no safe space to meet in a community setting that is not affiliated with an agency or church—institutions that are often unacceptable to adolescents and young adults, who don't find them "cool."

In addition to logistical concerns there are other, more substantive reasons why many social agencies do not consider groups a preferable treatment mode. There is the question of the availability of practitioners who are proficient in group skills, since many practitioners have worked mostly with individual client systems.

GROUPS AS INTERVENTION OF CHOICE WITH OVERWHELMED POPULATIONS

In the following chapters we intend to show that groups constitute an intervention of choice for work with oppressed populations. We argue that preparing practitioners to be skillful in group intervention with this population should become a priority for the helping professions. The sense of empowerment that clients derive from group experiences should be more highly respected and valued. Groups should not be seen, as so often is the case, as detracting from the highly valued one-on-one clinical modality, but as a compelling addition to the total helping repertoire.

2

A CONCEPTUAL FRAMEWORK FOR GROUP INTERVENTION WITH OVERWHELMED CLIENTS

The clients described in this book have been overwhelmed by poverty, racism, depression, the consequences of immigrant status, substance abuse, and the presence of HIV/AIDS in a family member. The group approaches that were used helped these clients who were entrapped by the consequences of one or more of these conditions to cope with them. Such intervention is consistent with the notion of empowerment that seeks not merely to eliminate symptoms but to change clients' sense of powerlessness including their entrapment in powerless societal roles. Empowerment requires a multileveled stance, which means that intervention takes place on individual, group, and/or community levels. The use of group strategies for empowerment is particularly effective since the group process, by its very nature, constitutes a vehicle for change on more than a single level. In this analysis we identify the conceptual framework and show its application to a variety of cases. The concepts are brought alive here primarily through the examples of two groups: Women Moving Forward and The Parenting Group for Recovering Addict Mothers. Other groups will also be examined in this book, as well as examples in the literature to broaden understanding. Embracing the goal of empowerment, the examples cited here illustrate change not merely in functioning on individual intrapsychic and interpersonal-interactive levels but also on the level of larger systems. They depict newer models of group intervention, particularly with overwhelmed clients, which look beyond personal change as the means of helping people to cope with the awesome realities they face. Such intervention involves attention to client and other systems functioning in terms of social role, social status, and even political process. Empowering clients from this multilevel perspective requires a conceptual framework that explains how power and lack of power operate on the various levels of human functioning and identifies the skills that practitioners need to facilitate clients' coping capacities.

POWER DYNAMICS: POWERLESSNESS AND POWER IN HUMAN BEHAVIOR

Power and lack of power are part of a multilevel systemic, sometimes contradictory, phenomenon that exists on all levels of human functioning. Pervasive though it is in the interactive behavior of people, power has remained a dirty word, avoided until recently as a focus in intervention. Power may be defined as the capacity to influence for one's own benefit the forces that affect one's life space, the capacity to produce desired effects on others. It is essential to mental health to feel some reasonable control over one's destiny and the forces that control one's life. Lack of power is painful and people seek to avoid such a state by behaving in ways that will turn their sense of powerlessness into a sense of power.[1] Having or lacking this necessary sense of power takes many forms for, as noted earlier, power is a key factor in functioning from the individual level, where "submission to power is . . . the earliest and most formative experience in human life,"[2] to the levels of family, group, and society.

Power exists on an internal-individual level in terms of mastery or competence; on an interactional level in terms of dominance-subordination; on a group and family level in terms of status, leadership, influence, and decision making; on an institutional level in terms of authority; and on a societal level in terms of group status and political action. The existence or nonexistence of power on any one of these levels can affect and be affected by its existence on any or all others. Moreover, while power exists in terms of oppression-victimization and dominance-subordination in relationships, it also exists as a circular, systemic process that is marked by reciprocity and symmetry where power is manifest in terms of equality. When relationships are reciprocal, roles are characterized by interdependence, equal and full participation, and collaboration, all of which enhance cohesiveness, a critical factor in the group's success. We observed these dynamics clearly in several groups and we will discuss the process by which the groups reached this cohesiveness and how practitioners facilitated this movement.

Practitioners who work with overwhelmed clients must understand the multileveled systemic nature of power as it operates in the larger social system, particularly because their clients often occupy powerless roles on more than one level. Practitioners, however, must also be aware of the consequences for themselves as helpers and for their relationship with clients. The helper role is automatically endowed with power—to assess and intervene; to teach and treat; to give and withhold resources. This power is compounded when the practitioner belongs to a dominant group (such as white, middle- or upper-class) because (1) that status is aggrandized in society and (2) such status embodies a benefit which allows members of the dominant group to reduce tension and anxiety in themselves and to achieve a sense of comfort by perceiving victim groups (such as minorities and the poor) as inferior and incompetent.[3] Members of dominant, beneficiary groups who work with overwhelmed clients occupying powerless societal roles thus can exploit their aggrandized social group status, relieving anxiety and reducing tension for themselves *whenever they work with persons from these victim groups.* Exploitation occurs whenever the practitioner behaves in ways that perpetuate clients' aggrandized perceptions of the practitioner while reinforcing clients' views of themselves as less valued, incompetent, and/or powerless.

This is true also for practitioners who are members of victim groups.

They too are vulnerable to exploiting clients if they seek to use the power that is embodied in their helping role to compensate for the powerlessness they experience in relation to their social roles.

Responses to Lacking Power: The Impact of Poverty and Class Status

Because the problems which clients bring are often closely connected with their powerless social roles on a variety of levels, practitioners need to understand how people behave when they lack power and are used as tension relievers, anxiety reducers, and victims of the social system. They use responses which they think will provide them with some sense of power. For example, our chapter on gang youth shows the extreme efforts these youth engage in to gain power. No one would argue their lack of success, at least in the short run. These responses which clients use and which enable them to survive are well known to practitioners who often see these behaviors as only pathological and not also survival based. Such behaviors will be seen in members of several of the groups we examine. For example, the men in the Parenting Group for Recovering Addict Fathers had used addiction and abusive behavior to cope with their entrapment in powerless societal roles. Of note is how possessive these fathers were of their children despite their tenuous and marginal connections to the children. Their actions toward their mates, companions, and/or their children's mothers were often abusive because they felt powerless when the mothers withheld visitation rights to the children, whom they often saw as their "only" possession and only achievement.

Other responses that people develop to cope with powerless roles also need understanding. These include being guarded (seen by the powerful as having lack of trust, or even being paranoid); persistently taking the initiative (seen as being oppositional, passive-aggressive) or being autonomous (seen by the powerful as being stubborn); and being manipulative, using avoidance and escape through alcohol and drugs. For many, guns constitute the ultimate power. Striking back has been a primary response in the cases we presented here since it is a common solution for coping with the pain of entrapment in the powerless roles that characterize much inner city life. Additional coping behaviors include assuming the projections forced upon them by society, for example, behaving as incompetent, dumb, crazy, supersexual, dependent, or addicted. (see Table 2–1).

While many individuals caught in these powerless roles refuse to embrace such stereotypes, others react by assuming these projections. Dependency, for example, becomes a strategy for getting a sense of power, since it enables one to be close to persons who do have power. Sometimes these behaviors are assumed in an exaggerated way which facilitates a feeling that one is an initiator rather than a victim.

Other related behaviors that have facilitated survival for those populations and can be understood as responses to entrapping societal roles include the use of competitive behaviors, put-downs and negativity, and the overvaluing toughness and struggle. These behaviors will be seen in the University Women of African Descent group where members used put-down responses to others and whose relational entanglements blocked their best academic performance. Another example will be seen in the Women Moving Forward group and in the way Lena, Tanya, and Della described the behavior of their male friends and husbands. These men had responded to their own entrapment in powerless social roles by a vulnerability to feeling put down or "dissed" (disrespected) by others. They then reacted defensively by using power-over, dominating behavior such as striking back, physical abuse, and the like. We will also see these dynamics in gang behavior where illegal and destructive empowerment is sought to cope with powerlessness on individual, family, and neighborhood levels.

These behaviors, which must be understood by social workers as survival responses to the powerlessness engendered by environmental pressures and powerless roles, are too often ignored, or seen merely as signs of deficiency.[4] However, although these behaviors are survival-based and bring some sense of power, they are also reactive and become extremely costly. Thus, persons who use these behaviors exclusively are severely handicapped. They cannot be proactive because they are trapped in reactive behaviors. They cannot be reciprocal in their relationships because they tend to view interaction in terms of dominance/subordination. When these behaviors become

TABLE 2–1

Frequently Described Feelings and Behaviors Related to Differences in Power

FEELINGS

View of the More Powerful	*View of the Less Powerful*
Having some comfort, more gratification	Having less comfort, less gratification
Feeling lucky, safe, and secure	Feeling insecure, anxious, frustrated, vulnerable
Experiencing more pleasure, less pain	Experiencing less pleasure, more pain
Having less tendency to depression	Having strong tendency to depression
Feeling superior, masterful, entitled	Feeling inferior, incompetent, deprived
Feeling hopeful	Feeling exhausted, trapped, hopeless, helpless, with few choices
Having high esteem	Having low esteem
Feeling anger at noncompliance	Feeling anger at inconsiderate control of the less powerful
Having fear of the loss of power by the powerful	Feeling anger at feelings of powerlessness
Having fear of the anger of less powerful	Having fear of abandonment
Having fear of retaliation by the less powerful	Feeling alone
Having guilt over injustices	Having fear of the anger of the powerful
Having fear of losing identity as a powerful person	Having fear of own anger at the powerful
Having a sense of burden of responsibility	Feeling the burden of the responsibility to survive
Having fear of abusing power	Feeling the abuse of the powerful

BEHAVIOR

Having the opportunity to impact the external system	Lacking opportunity to impact the external system or self
Having ability to create opportunity	Lacking ability to create opportunity
Having ability to take responsibility	Lacking ability to take responsibility
Exerting responsibility	Not exerting responsibility
Projecting on the less powerful unacceptable attributes, such as being lazy, dirty, evil, sexual, and irresponsible, as justification for maintaining power and control	Projecting onto the power group acceptable attributes, such as being smart, competent, attractive, moral, as justification for having power and control

Blaming the less powerful for assuming suffering

Devaluing one's own pain and the projections of suffering

Having distrust, being guarded and rigid due to vigilance needed to maintain power and control

Having distrust, being guarded and sensitive to discrimination, often seeming paranoid to the power group

Denying the powerful position and its favorable effects on beneficiaries and unfavorable effects on victims

Denying the less powerful position and its effects on victims

Displaying a paranoia resulting in delusions of acceptance, superiority, grandiosity, unrealistic sense of entitlement

Displaying a paranoia resulting in the sense of a dependent position, passivity, and the assumption of arrogant behavior, and tendency to distort stereotypes, such as a physical or stud image, reality with a consequent unreal assessment of the self and dumbness, delinquency, and addiction, with the consequent unreal less powerful assessment of oneself and the more powerful

Isolating, avoiding, and distancing from the less powerful

Isolating, avoiding, and distancing from the more powerful

Taking comfort in sameness; becoming unable to tolerate differences in people; and lacking enriching cross-cultural experiences

Discomfort with financial differences; comfort with cultural differences

Displaying entitled, controlling, dominating behavior

Utilizing autonomous, oppositional, manipulative, and passive-aggressive behavior as a defense against powerlessness

Displaying rigidity in behavior: have to keep the sense of control

Displaying rigidity in behavior: to control sense of powerlessness

Having a need for a victim, someone to scapegoat and control

Striking out, becoming verbally or physically aggressive to ward off powerlessness

Justifying aggression, and exertion of power or violence; dehumanizing behavior, and pleasure at suffering

Self-devaluation; aggressive, violent behavior

Identifying with the less powerful, leading to a wish to repudiate power

Identifying with the aggressor, leading to self-hatred

Use of deceptions, secrets, half-truths, lies

(continued)

TABLE 2–1 *continued*

Projecting aggression outside the group onto the less powerful to enhance group cohesiveness and unity	Projecting aggression outside the group onto the more powerful to enhance group cohesiveness and unity
(This behavior is assisted by a sense of entitlement.)	(This behavior is reinforced by a sense of justice.)
Experiencing conflict and confusion resulting from (1) a sense of injustice versus a need to hold on to the power and (2) a wish to share the power versus the fear of rejection by one's own ethnic group	

SHARING POWER

Turning powerlessness into power	Turning reactive power into proactive power which constitutes second order change
Developing a tolerance for conflict ambivalence and contradiction which, when mastered, leads to flexibility, resourcefulness, creativity, and high self-esteem	Developing a tolerance for conflict ambivalence and contradiction which, when mastered, leads to flexibility, resourcefulness, creativity, and high self-esteem
	Becoming aware of one's own power and how to use it
	Taking action to change the social structures that block being able to control own destiny
	Creating and building own supportive networks
	Working together in a group and with others outside of group who share own situation to create change.

Source: Adapted from E. Pinderhughes (1989), *Understanding Race, Ethnicity and Power: Key to Efficacy in Clinical Practice*, New York: Free Press.

predominant, people are not able to set their own goals or course of action because they are trapped in responding to the agenda and initiatives of others. Such behaviors thus do not help them achieve their own goals. For example, though successful and spunky, the University Women of African Descent found themselves entrapped in reactive behavior that interfered with their intended goals. Such behaviors by the members of the groups we examine here prevented them from developing a sense of mastery over life.[5] Reactive behaviors, including striking back and being violent—including being murderously violent—could only temporarily ease their sense of powerlessness and bring a sense of domination momentarily. And the power such behavior conveys is not only fleeting but false because it will readily mobilize retaliation from the other party, thus creating even greater powerlessness and entrapment in what easily becomes an escalating systemic process.

In summary, these dynamics are concepts that have relevance for all persons intending to take responsibility for managing responses to personal entrapment in systemic processes and seeking to interact comfortably with others. They have relevance for victims who would change their powerless roles so that they can have control over significant aspects of their lives.

Responses to Having Power: The Impact of Privilege

The dynamics of power and powerlessness also have relevance for those who, as beneficiaries in the societal process, occupy power-assigned roles, such as that of the white male and, more relevant to this discussion, the practitioner, leader, politician, or the like—roles requiring those who take them to control their personal vulnerability to the handicapping consequences of the privilege that they embody. For example, if they allow themselves they can, as a result of these privileged roles, develop a sense of entitlement, a prejudiced perspective of others, a distorted perspective of themselves, and, in the extreme, they can be trapped in paranoid thinking, paralyzing guilt, immobilizing fear, and a readiness to exploit or benefit from their power position.[6]

Persons who have power experience it as gratifying and pleasurable. They are able to affect systems and create opportunities for themselves, to take responsibility and exert leadership (see Table 2–1). However, they may also be fearful of those who are powerless or especially of losing their power, becoming angry and/or feeling guilty. Having the power to define the powerless, people in power also can project onto the powerless their own responses to repressed internal needs, which are then perceived as existing in the powerless.[7] They can use these projections to provide justification for maintaining power and control over their victims, and ultimately then blame the powerless for assuming these projections.

Practitioners must understand these dynamics and exercise their own power to empower clients. They must understand client survival behaviors as attempts to cope with powerless societal conditions. They should be capable of helping clients understand the reactive, self-defeating nature of such behavior and able to model and teach clients new empowering behaviors that are nondominating and more collaborative.

INTERVENTION: EMPOWERMENT PRINCIPLES
INVOLVING CONTEXT

Recently there has been recognition that using groups merely to produce growth-enhancing insight and knowledge is insufficient. It is also important that goal setting, discussion, and planning result in action. An action orientation means that group members will hold each other accountable to the expectation that all members will go beyond their comfort zone to making life-enhancing choices oriented toward truth, dignity, integrity, honesty, and courage.[8] Reid[9] notes that it is important for the group to assess actions taken irrespective of outcome. It is also important to examine within the group all anticipated actions to safeguard against unwise moves. This involves identifying reactive behaviors, distorted thinking, misunderstanding, and confusion, and also requires guidance regarding mobilizing and identifying feelings of anger so that they can be better managed and will not constitute blocks to effective action.

Starting with a group of mothers, Women Moving Forward, we will see individuals becoming empowered as they unloaded their burdens, reframed their perspective on their conditions, their rights and realities, and reframed their options in the light of these new realities while looking for routes to growth. During this process of unburdening and unloading we see how the members moved to their support. This happened in differing degrees in all of the groups. Such an outcome might have been achieved in individual therapy but we doubt that it would have occurred as fast. Efforts by members to offer support as they held each other accountable to their goals were significant factors.

Empowerment and action to change powerless roles give attention not only to individual, interactive functioning but also, as noted earlier, to social role, social status, and political process as foci for change. These aspects of larger societal functioning must now be included in the intervention endeavor as areas for the group to examine and to act on. In this approach, client problems are contextualized. Strategies are used that help clients to connect their specific problem or need to the social context. An example is the Vietnamese women's group. Yet another example is the Syracuse gang intervention program. What we see is that problems are examined in terms of how they have been influenced by larger system processes such as racism, gender-role expectations, and the denigrated identities and oppressed statuses that have been central to the realities which clients face.

The use of such strategies reinforces clients' strengths so that they come to recognize how the solutions they have sought to their problems show how hard they have struggled to deal with the contradictions and powerless roles they have been trapped in. They understand that the maneuvers they have chosen represent the natural wish of everyone to be strong and to cope effectively with powerless, stressful societal roles. For example, parents at risk of using abusive disciplinary practices can be helped to see that they use such practices because they are exhausted, overwhelmed, and desperate to make their children behave. This strategy of relabeling, as family therapists well understand, deals effectively with the ambivalence and contradiction that are universally experienced by societal victims.

Managing Survival Behaviors

Thus a mother who lacks support systems and is struggling alone, and who compensates by becoming controlling, overly central, and smothering in relating to her children, can learn that her heroic efforts to organize the family are exhausting her. A mother who is neglecting her family can be told that she has given up on being in charge because she feels overwhelmed, confused, and defeated. An overfunctioning father who is seen as too authoritative and controlling can learn that his heroic efforts to provide for and protect his family in the face of disorganizing, supportive, often racist "support systems" have been necessary but are interfering with his children's growth. Many of these behaviors were seen in the Recovering Addict Mothers' group and the Recovering Addict Fathers' group where such functioning was identified and confronted through different phases of the group process. An underfunctioning father can be told that backing off may be his way of reducing stress in the family. Underfunctioning becomes a strategy to keep peace, avoid conflict, reduce stress, promote harmony/connectedness, and/or protect family members. However, that father should understand that his family needs him; thus his struggle to survive and manage the systemic confusion and contradiction in which he is trapped must be validated by the practitioner.

In each of the group examples here, with the exception of the privileged mixed gender group, it was necessary for the practitioner to address personal, individual, and systemic structural deficits such as income, housing, health, school, day care, and camp in addition to personal deficits such as substance abuse and depression. In the mixed gender group where group members were largely middle class and white, the practitioners focused primarily on personal deficits—substance abuse, poor relationships, and so forth.

In addressing these multilevel deficits, support and information were given. For example, in the parents' groups, members learned about child development, what to expect of a child, how to manage specific problems, and how to set personal behavior goals such as managing anger and reducing stress. Attention and activity were directed to the environmental lacks that had created or compounded clients' problems. And a major objective was to understand that their ways of responding to their awesome realities were actually attempts to be strong and to cope. They learned to see how striking back or antisocial behaviors can be tied to a false sense of pride or a reactive sense of power. The fathers' parenting group is an example that illustrates these strategies. These clients, depressed from entrapment in societal processes, were in danger of abusing their children or partners. As former victims of drug abuse, they needed to develop new and expanded awareness of themselves and their environment. They needed to see how their personal contribution to their problems interfaced with larger system processes to keep them entrapped. We are reminded that this dynamic was also manifest in the university women's group.

Some of the empowerment strategies that are used with the overwhelmed population are based on cognitive-behavioral approaches. These approaches seek to teach clients how to exercise power effectively and change their problem-compounding, maladaptive behavior and cognitive sets. Using education strategies invokes a lower power differential in the helper-client relationship than does the use of counseling and therapeutic strategies. Teaching clients how to exercise power effectively can be accomplished by role playing, modeling, and coaching them on how to behave appropriately in a role that requires authority and being in charge (such as parent or community leader). Since their struggles to survive in these powerless roles have pushed them to embrace survival behaviors that may cause them even more problems, such people want and need to learn how to exercise power appropriately and effectively. For example, an African-American battered woman does "not find that her partner's violence is her main concern, nor her worst oppressor"[10] and therefore clings to her mate. An impoverished mother uses physical punishment such as spanking and demands absolute obedience because, stressed out, she feels she has no time or energy to punish her child by withdrawing love as do middle-class mothers. She also has no money to reward good behavior by bestowing material rewards. However, practitioners who would teach such a mother new and more effective ways to exert appropriate power must work hard to understand her perceptions of her realities. Instruction in how to be appropriately authoritative must not devalue this mother's struggles to cope.

When clients are helped to understand that these responses are related to their attempts to survive their powerless roles, they can learn that their attempts to feel strong and to cope can even include assuming, to an extreme, the negative attributions and stereotypes of the larger society. They come to see that, as we noted earlier, the sense of being strong which they get from such exaggerated behavior comes from the fact that they think they are exercising initiative. They can also learn that turning around the meaning of the negative labels which people give them is another means of being strong and of surviving. Such maneuvers seek to transform impotence into an active force: since one cannot stop others from identifying oneself by a negative label, one can empower oneself by changing its meaning. In this context, such behaviors as those described above are adaptive.

When clients can understand that neither they nor their adaptive mechanisms are at fault, they can see that it is the degree to which they have embraced these survival strategies that is the problem. For under stress, adaptability can easily slip into inconsistency, toughness and strength into abuse, persistence into stubbornness, caution into immobilization, and hard work into overdriven dedication. Examples from the groups demonstrate the degree to which group members were vulnerable to engage in these behaviors as part of their struggles to cope.

Intervention strategies that are based on these dynamics will also focus on new, more empowering behaviors for clients. But first they must recognize that the behaviors which they have used in their determination to be strong and to cope with the powerlessness embodied in their roles can exact a high price even though they have eased the sense of entrapment. For example, the need to always be in control and strike back is costly because it can keep power struggles going and reinforce a power stance where one feels one has to win, be in charge, put others down, and even resort to violence. Having to win does not support the problem-solving or reciprocal behavior that is needed for harmonious, cohesive relationships. Moreover, exaggerated autonomy, which does help one to make it by oneself when there appears to be no help, can mean being unable to use help even when it is available.

In the overwhelmed groups, with the exception of the Vietnamese women, it was important for practitioners to help members learn to be democratic and to moderate their controlling behavior. This was seen most clearly in the Recovering Addict Fathers' Group. These clients needed to recognize that they were being reactive—that they were always responding to somebody else's initiative. They needed to learn how to be proactive, to respond to their own initiatives, and to avoid "power-over" behaviors as new ways to be strong. They learned to see that setting and pursuing goals and being assertive in ways that did not reinforce power over relationships, put others down, or keep power struggles going, could be a different way of being strong. This behavior, like the ability to negotiate and compromise, was not reactive. Making the decision not to escalate a battle, but rather to allow oneself to take a one-down position and to be vulnerable, is also a way of taking initiative and at the same time showing strength. Indeed, learning to function in a proactive way and developing a tolerance for vulnerability can be important acquisitions for persons whose survival strategies have pushed them to become rigidly defensive and power oriented. Furthermore, learning to negotiate, compromise, and tolerate vulnerability in relationships facilitates a capacity for connectedness to others and guards against disconnection and isolation.

We call attention to how turning around conflict-laden behaviors became a priority goal in the Recovering Addict Fathers' Group and how the practitioner used role playing, talking through, and rehearsal to help members develop new ways of dialoguing with their women and their children. These fathers learned to frame their requests to the women in their lives without criticism and attack, to communicate with respect, and to omit swearing and abusive behavior. It was hard work for all.

These new prosocial behaviors that must be taught to group members contrast sharply with the antisocial behavior which clients have used in the past. The sense of power which these new behaviors embody will not cause greater problems but will bring members closer to the goals they seek. These behaviors are of course best learned when the helping relationship itself models collaterality and client participation as was the case in the groups examined.

The Practitioner

The group leader must have a mastery of power dynamics in order to manifest the skills that are necessary for facilitating empowerment. Many of the strategies needed to empower clients involve the skilled and appropriate use of a nonhierarchical, nonpower stance on the part of the practitioner, particularly after the early phases of intervention. The leader stance in empowerment models is not that of a manipulator but of a partner, facilitator, and/or collaborator who "does with" rather than "to" or "for." The power of the leader vis-à-vis the group's members is far less than that which exists in individual work or even in traditional therapeutic group process. The functions of facilitator, mediator, perspective provider, and stimulator become catalysts for emergence of the power which clients possess but can not yet use. Employing interaction and exchange, functioning with interdependence, mutuality, and ongoing connectedness are important behaviors for group members. They are fully as important as independence and self-sufficiency.[11] These nonpower behaviors are also critical for leaders. McGowan[12] suggests that practitioners' readiness to use a nonpower stance is often compromised. Commenting on the need for such a nonhierarchical, nonpower stance with some clients as revealed in her research, McGowan notes that such a stance is difficult for many practitioners because they are deprived "of many of their customary protections, myths and sources of individual satisfaction."[13] Pointing to the displeasure expressed by these practitioners despite their avowal of the importance of such stance and procedures, she notes that "they found it difficult to experience the loss of control that is inevitable."[14] Giving up control or sharing control with the client may be threatening. Imber-Black comments:

> It is not unusual to behold clients who struggle with their workers, attempting to bid for a more collaborative relationship, marked by a sense of personal empowerment and workers who insist on maintaining the complementary arrangement, as this often provides their only sense of empowerment, however tenuous.[15]

However, regardless of the levels of functioning that do become the target of change in the empowerment process, practitioners' readiness to empower clients depends on their capacity to manage their own personal power needs. Knowledge of these needs and responses is critical to the self-knowledge they must have. This is because the sense of power or mastery that is critical for mental health exists for practitioners and clients alike. And for practitioners, as well as clients, that sense of power can affect or be affected by the presence or absence of power in other areas of their lives and/or other levels of functioning. At the same time practitioners are also automatically endowed with the power that is implicit in the helper role: the power to assess and intervene, to teach and treat, to give or withhold resources. Thus it is important that practitioners understand how the power embodied in their helping role can be and too often has been exploited to meet their own needs for power and esteem.[16] The rapid escalation in situations being reported where practitioners have sexually abused their patients/clients illustrates this potential. Practitioner power used to bolster the image of the practitioner constitutes perhaps the most infamous of practitioner abuses.[17]

In the helping encounter where client and practitioner are from different backgrounds and statuses, this already automatic liability to exploitation is compounded. The power associated with the practitioners' role may be compounded by the aggrandizement that is associated with their social/cultural groups, and practitioner vulnerability to use this power in order to satisfy personal need is far greater than one may think. The significance of this for the helping endeavor is explained by Murray Bowen's concept as discussed earlier. As noted, this process suggests that the dominant group in a society can, through projection upon a less powerful group (victims), relieve anxiety and reduce tension in itself, thereby improving its functioning.

In the helping encounter, thus, practitioners who are members of dominant, beneficiary groups (white, male, middle- or upper-class, or other high-status groups) can exploit their aggrandized social/cultural group status, relieving anxiety and reducing tension for themselves whenever they work with persons from victim groups (people of color, poor, female, or other groups with low status assignment). Exploitation occurs whenever practitioners engage in behavior that perpetuates clients' aggrandized perception of the practitioner as powerful and expert while facilitating clients' perception of themselves as less valued, incompetent, and powerless. Intervention is only truly successful when these perceptions by clients of themselves are changed and they learn to see themselves as peers who are competent persons of value. Practitioners who are ethnic people of color or gay or who are members of other oppressed social groups are not exonerated from this vulnerability. They too are vulnerable to exploiting clients if they cannot manage appropriately their negative responses to their own victim group membership. They are, indeed, vulnerable to using the power embodied in their helping role to compensate for the powerlessness they may experience in relation to their social role. This is a place where much stuckness and conflict can occur in relationships and in practice. When people from power groups attempt to point out such behavior on the part of persons belonging to victim groups, they may be perceived by these "victims" as attacking and racist.

Understanding the dynamics of power in the helping process, and their influence upon the meaning to practitioners of their own social/cultural identity, helps guard against client exploitation. Being able to examine these liabilities and to understand the purpose of the behaviors that create them facilitates ability to control them. To understand the dynamics of power in relation to race, ethnicity, gender, and class identity, they need to give special attention to self-examination in these areas.

Such self-examination requires practitioners to consider how the societal projection process provides a sense of competence, stability, and lack of confusion for them as benefactor-beneficiaries while it reinforces anxiety and greater confusion for victims (their clients). They must also ask themselves whether and under what circumstances they, as helpers working with persons from victim groups, do in fact receive gratification from their helper role. They need to acknowledge when they are, in fact, in a double power role with their clients, and examine how such vulnerability may threaten the helping process. They must question whether the goals they are pursuing and the strategies they are using are influenced by personal need for the gratification that is embodied in their powerful professional and societal roles. They must see clearly their own entrapment in the societal projection process and, facing their vulnerability to exploitation of those roles, they must take responsibility for managing any behaviors that result.

If practitioners are uncomfortable about not being in control, if

they look for aggrandizement in relation to their social/cultural identity, or to any other powerful societal role, the ability to relinquish control and to practice the reciprocity, mutuality, and self-disclosure so
necessary for effectiveness with many clients will be compromised. It is
only when practitioners' power needs are under control that they can
value their clients' strengths, take one-down positions when appropriate, and respect cultural meaning that may be different from their own.
Again, the example of Betty's first group experience with a leader who
exploited his powerful practitioner role is instructive.

Practitioners' flexibility in thinking and/or behavior facilitates the
capacity to adapt their work styles to the values, expectations, and pref-
erences of their diverse client population. With such flexibility they
can work effectively even if the values underlying these expected behaviors are vastly different from their own and from those that have
been the foundation for traditional assessment and treatment approaches. The extra steps and additional energy required to exercise
this needed flexibility will not overwhelm them, lead them to defensively distort their clients' responses and experiences, or devalue the
activity that is needed to engage the client in order to intervene appropriately. Neither will they abandon the effort.

When aware of their own power needs and responses and familiar
with their internalized responses to difference, practitioners are more
able to manage these and are less threatened when strategies are called
for that require them to function in a less hierarchical, more power-
sharing mode. Because they are comfortable with being vulnerable,
they can more easily engage in the mutuality, reciprocity, capacity for
openness, and self-disclosure that are expected by clients who belong
to certain cultural groups. These behaviors are generally consistent
with the cultural values and expectations of Native Americans and
some Puerto Ricans and African-Americans. For example, research
shows that it is critical to be open and to self-disclose with African-
Americans. Asians, in contrast, are more likely to expect authoritative,
directive approaches.

Power-sharing modes may also be necessary for work with clients
whose experiences with personal and social powerlessness have been
such that they cannot be engaged, and cannot begin to change their

collusion with their own victimization without the use of strategies that give them some sense of power. Training thus will help practitioners to become comfortable with strategies emphasizing collaboration and client equal participation. Practitioners will be prepared to dialogue with clients as peers, and to engage in the "power with" rather than "power over" behaviors required in the new empowerment models that are now rapidly appearing on the scene.[18] At the same time, their capacity for flexibility will also enable them to be directive and authoritative when appropriate.

With training practitioners can begin to exercise these skills. Their negative responses to difference from others will be under firm control, and they will be ready to manage any personal discomfort related to anxiety about difference or power need. They will not automatically view their client's adaptations, whether they are culturally based or whether they constitute responses to oppression, as signs of pathology or incompetence. They will be on guard against the need to employ stereotypes (which are in themselves anxiety-reducing mechanisms) or to cast their clients' reference groups in images of weakness, dependency, dysfunction, and pathology.

Because they are free to see their culturally and socially different clients in the context of their environment, practitioners with the needed self-knowledge can more easily view their clients as unknowledgeable or blocked from access, as trapped in positions where environmental insufficiency becomes a factor in the etiology of the problem and in the solutions that should be sought. They are thus readier to focus on clients' strengths and believe in their clients' potential. In *The Power to Care* we noted that high expectations of clients trapped in transgenerational poverty are a major factor in successful outcome: "In fact the best predictor of successful client change is flexible and caring practitioners who in their practice expose clients to high goals and expect them to rise to the occasion."[19] When well prepared, practitioners believe in their clients' capacity to exercise power and their readiness to mobilize it. They can also reinforce clients' perceptions of themselves as collaborators and as persons of value who belong to a group that has value and whose members are capable and competent to function as change agents for themselves. These behaviors constitute true empowerment. When practitioners facilitate client actions that are based on these perceptions, changes in clients' powerless roles become inevitable.

A GROUP FOR PROJECT MOTHERS: WOMEN MOVING FORWARD

The following example is offered as an illustration of these empowerment concepts. The group, Women Moving Forward, was offered in an agency that actually attempted to address the need for neighborhood empowerment and growth, thereby effecting change on both individual and societal levels. The example describes empowerment techniques such as the use of support, enhancing client self-differentiation, and the capacity to manage power over defensive behavior. This outreach approach is completely devoid of any labeling, pathology focus on the families and mothers in the group. Understanding that the needs of community residents were both personal and socioeconomic, the agency employed several indigenous residents in clerical and outreach positions, encouraging them to use their knowledge of the environment and of families to engage in aggressive but culturally sensitive contact with a nearby housing project.

Primary among the concerns identified in the needs assessment undertaken by the staff were those of the children. Health and school officials also were concerned about the children and supported the agency's community-based intervention focus. Activities were started using a combination of recreational and psycho-educational approaches. Children came to the center in response to flyers posted in hallways of the project where they all lived and also in response to telephone calls to their residences. In a few instances mothers dropped their children off, but more often they drifted in alone. One youngster stated that he came to the center "because I'm scared." It doesn't take a lot of advertisement to draw in children who are afraid and want protection, or who are idle, with little access to enriching and nurturing activities. Good snacks, bright colorful play space, and engaging, friendly, energetic staff helped.

As the children became more involved in activities practitioners learned more about them, their families, and their day-to-day struggles. Who was getting evicted, whose parents were fighting all the time and on the verge of breaking up, who got hit by cops for drugs, and what family was coping with a daughter's unexpected pregnancy were bits of information that were passed around.

One afternoon a youth told about being approached to buy drugs from a white pusher "who used black talk." According to his story, he and his friends ganged up and ran the pusher out of a local fast food gathering place.

Practitioners also heard about child-rearing practices and what children were spanked, slapped, and left alone without supervision. They became aware also that some families enjoyed supports and seemed to benefit from extended family—for example, some children had an opportunity to travel with a grandmother to visit relatives in another town or for shopping trips downtown or to a mall. It was clear that some children belonged to families whose connections were healthy and intact while others were only marginally connected, cut off, or even isolated. These dynamics were compounded for immigrant children who experienced bewildering ambiguity and confusion stemming from their lack of knowledge and understanding of life in a new country.

Fighting at the slightest provocation was a behavioral response for some of the children. Why? For others aggression and violence were described as a way of communication. A two-and-a-half-year-old, for example, angered by her mother's refusal to give her a piece of candy, screamed, "Do you want me to open up your face?" Another youngster, who was burdened with a family secret concerning her family's survival, was obsessed with the fear that the secret would be revealed by a friend with whom she had discussed it. Especially if secrets relate to such survival issues as illegal immigration or political refugee status, they can constitute "life and death" issues. Families who hide relatives feel vulnerable to risk and forbid children from talking about it. When a family's code of silence is broken by a child, and its safety jeopardized, the consequences can result in very rough discipline and abusive management. Similar burdens are experienced by large numbers of children who live in families where there are problems with sexual abuse, domestic violence, and drugs.

Gradually the practitioners gained more knowledge about families struggling with such issues as they increasingly came in contact with parents who appeared to collect their children from agency-sponsored activities. These practitioners helped arrange medical assistance for families, or intervened with the housing project management on their behalf. Over time some parents could see the benefits accruing to their children and became supportive of such programs. Practitioners surmised that parents who seemed uninterested feared that engagement might bring more risks because of their lifestyles—drugs, gang involvement, pushing—although a few did allow their children to attend activities sponsored by the agency.

Thus, parents became involved with the agency through their children, and the open reception they received encouraged their dropping in, chatting, and visiting with staff. Openness, moving at clients' pace, and showing respect by listening to their complaints—especially about the conditions in the project—were reflective of the agency's philosophy and expectations of staff. Some recent immigrants, for example, were encouraged by these strategies to feel welcome and gradually connections to the agency and practitioners developed. "Welcome" posters in English and Spanish were positive signals that the agency and staff were there for clients.

Space for parents to drop in and have a cup of tea or coffee meant there was a place for time away from a hectic or disorganized home, and/or a welcome place to browse through newspapers and magazines—expensive items for poor families—and discuss ever-pressing concerns with someone or get help reading and interpreting documents. The realization that a shared group experience would be beneficial and, therefore, welcome was a slowly evolving process.

Six mothers gathered in response to outreach from agency practitioners regarding a mothers' group for support of the children's activities. Initially the group focused on the structured activities offered by the agency to children. Do the children like the playground? The reading hour? The snacks? What should be changed? (Interestingly, in the children's reading hour, one book, *Mommy, What Is Drunk?*, had a significant effect on parent motivation to use the center. One youngster took the book home and shared it with her father, who, having been resistant to family involvement at the center, now encouraged his children's participation.)

All of these mothers, primarily young adults in their early 20s, were poor, single parents struggling with problems such as joblessness, lack of standard housing, and parenting issues. All were African-American, though an effort was made to include white and Latino mothers. Several struggled with psychological and emotional issues related to past and current drug addiction and family relationships. They were still embroiled in unsettled bonding battles with their own mothers—that is, they were still struggling to become self-directed and self-responsible and comfortable with interdependency.

As the group progressed through the initial engagement and icebreaking phase, the focus shifted to the mothers themselves and some of their day-to-day reality problems. By this time, a certain degree of trust had been built. The mothers' complaints centered on housing deficiencies, money shortage, and inaccessibility of shopping locations for food and clothing. Since money was tight and transportation difficult, an idea suggested by the worker of organizing themselves into a buying club took hold. Transportation was supplied by the agency for weekly trips to supersaver markets, co-op markets, and food pantries. On the way to and from these stores they shared ideas regarding cooking, preparing meals, and bulk buying for economy. There was opportunity here for health-focused discussions: which foods are harmful and which ones promote better nutrition, how to serve healthy and more cost-effective meals.

They also planned a regular activity, the breakfast club, in which members met at a local restaurant once a month. It became a popular activity which attracted the full membership. Food-related activities generally hold significance for everyone; on a psychological level they symbolize nurturance and being cared about, especially for the emotionally hungry. Particularly for persons who have felt deprived of early emotional and psychological nurturing and supports, food can be turned to as a source of compensation.

Other activities the group planned included self-beautification and self-care. Members learned expert application of make-up, tried out exotic new hairstyles, and learned appropriate dress for different occasions. Goals here centered on building self-esteem and confidence: looking and feeling better was a goal. When it was discovered that one member of the group could not read (a fact which she had hidden carefully), literacy for all became a goal. The women named the group "Women Moving Forward," and were becoming more interested in participation in the planning and implementing of activities.

Later, child rearing and parenting with a focus on anger management also became group concerns. Gangs and drugs were not uncommon topics which on occasion created tension within the group because some members lived with or were involved with pushers. Indeed, hearing some members talk about the destructive side of drugs was stressful for those who were themselves using drugs and/or taking drug money from boyfriends/pushers to supplement their households.

Women Moving Forward: Lena, Tanya, and Della

After the group had met for about nine months a degree of trust developed that enabled members to begin sharing some of the painful psychological and emotional struggles occurring in their families. (Before this happened one member had announced her intent "not to talk about anything personal.") This type of movement was facilitated by support from the practitioner who sought to create an atmosphere of safety and openness that encouraged greater readiness to be vulnerable with one another. This atmosphere and the behavioral stance she encouraged reflect the view that all people are capable of sharing issues about their personal world in discussion and encounters with others if each group member can be helped to express herself in time and without fear or shame.

Lena, a 23-year-old mother of two girls, aged eight and six, and a boy aged five, began to share her problems with her alcohol-abusing unemployed boyfriend who took her money in order to buy liquor. For Lena and her children such a situation meant never having special treats like

a movie, a magazine, fresh fruit, or a trip to the mall for Chinese food or
pizza, but more than that, it meant deprivation of necessities. Whenever
Lena tried to resist giving up the money, her boyfriend became argumen-
tative and explosive. He swore, banged on doors, and threatened her and
the children, so that Lena, feeling helpless, powerless, and trapped, be-
came frightened and gave in to his demands.

This confusion and sense of helplessness led her to begin using the
drugs her boyfriend introduced her to, and resulted in another drain
on her limited financial and emotional resources. Lena struggled for
many months to become drug free. A major issue in her battle centered on her relationships with old friends who were still on drugs,
and the difficulty in maintaining the necessary distance from those relationships.

What am I going to do on Saturdays when my friends get high and go to
the mall, or when they get high and stay home and watch reruns of the
soaps? What will they say about me? They might not call me anymore.
How will they treat my children?

While Lena worked with her clinician on an individual basis to develop ways of thinking and behaving that would enable her to become
and remain drug free, the group helped fill the void in her life that she
felt after she gave up drugs and had to distance herself from her still
drugging friends. A significant factor in her successful outcome was the
support provided by the group. Supported by the practitioner and the
process of personal goal setting within the group, Lena struggled to understand why she needed this relationship with her drug-abusing
boyfriend, who was a "taker." Reflecting on their functioning, she said,
"My boyfriend is a child. I am the one who has to be responsible. He
needs to grow up."

In a later chapter we discuss the burdens carried by children
like Lena's and the pain and trauma experienced by many who are
exposed to the consequences of drugs, including seeing their mothers'
boyfriends beating them, taking their money, or forcing them to
have sex.

After much turmoil and some months of work Lena decided to end the relationship. Becoming very active in the group, she began to take responsibility for organizing the buying trips, encouraging other members to support the agency's youth activities, and helping members to open up, share concerns, and engage in dialogue about reasonable solutions. Her growth throughout this process was evident as she manifested strong relational skills and overall increased competency.

Tanya, 22, an active group member, discussed her hostile-dependent relationship with her mother. She stated:

My ma is always telling me 'bout myself. Nothing I do is right—I keep my house a mess, I ain't raising my kids right and my men are no good.

The two women battled constantly over what Tanya perceived as her mother's bossiness and control. Although she lived in her own apartment with her five-year-old twins she constantly manipulated her mother into caring for her out-of-wedlock children, preparing meals, helping with the cleaning, and buying groceries. Later it was revealed that Tanya herself was on drugs while she sought an escape from the overwhelming demands of motherhood which had begun at age 17. Tanya felt even more overwhelmed by her mother's anxiety about her addiction, promiscuity, and poor parenting skills and by the barrages of criticism with which it was communicated. Tanya was finally able to get beyond some of the battles with her mother, and with help from her clinician and support from the group she was able to secure a job and function more appropriately as a mother.

Della, age 28, had a handicapped ten-year-old son and two younger boys, eight and three. Talented in sewing and eager to learn dress design, she discussed her struggles to get a GED and her hope of going to a community college. Struggling to be responsible and better her circumstances, she seemed to have more familial support and emotional resources than the other two women. Also she had managed to be less entangled in a battling relationship with either a boyfriend or a parent. Della was able to reach her goal of getting a GED, and enrolled in a fashion design course at the community college. Later, she gave a fashion show, making the clothes herself and using her group sisters as models. Unfortunately her boyfriend returned and, threatened by her success, derailed her up-wardly mobile trajectory. Dropping out of college and the group, Della became seriously depressed again.

Through the group, the mothers managed to reduce their loneliness and social isolation, feeling that from day to day they were not in the boat alone. They learned to take advantage of many resources in the greater Boston metropolitan area, visiting parks and museums and attending cultural activities, experiences that would have been intimidating to a group member alone. One site that the members visited was the monument of Crispus Attucks, a black man who was the first casualty in the Revolutionary War, a fact the group members had not learned in school. At first their reaction was one of disbelief.

Another lesson learned was that there is power in numbers. They were not as powerless as they believed; they could take on, for example, the "front office" at the housing project and even think about how to mobilize resources in order to move out of public housing. Their sense of competence was reinforced as members functioned as consultants to one another about day-to-day problems, emotional stresses, and pain. During Lena's struggle with drugs, group members would often point out the destructiveness of her habit, why she needed to give up drugs, and how her kids needed her.

Sometimes progress in the group needed reinforcement through individual work outside of the group. In such cases it was important that an agreement be made to the effect that if the client felt an uncontrollable urge to drink or do drugs, she would immediately contact the practitioner. The practitioner would respond on the spot, and help the client, examining the incident that had provoked the urge to drink or snort. Usually this led to identifying some painful interaction or thought process relative to issues related to loss or abandonment. One member, describing what made her want a drink, stated: "I couldn't deal with my boyfriend putting me down. I needed a drink." Another commented, "My mother makes me drink."

Group members learned many lessons as they shared personal pain, offered each other mutual support, and developed skills in exercising democratic ideas about governance, lessons that were not without struggles and conflict. After several years Lena's growth and competence was such that she became a member of the staff. This happened at a time when staff and community had begun to recognize that the escalation of drug use necessitated some community focus. Lena helped to organize and conduct a drug awareness group. New clients found her a model of strength and understanding: a successful graduate from drugs, the welfare rolls, and public housing. Lena's transition from a powerless, drug-using, abused tenant to a respected, trusted indigenous practitioner is instructive. How did group processes facilitate this growth in Lena? What was the role of the practitioner? The other group members? And, what role did Lena herself play? We will examine techniques that were used to help members grow and change in Chapter 8.

The impressive change in Lena was difficult to bring about both inside and outside the group. Drawing on the expertise of the practitioner, a group leader who was competent in both group and individual modalities, Lena overcame her fear of rejection and abandonment by her group members and other friends whom she saw as jealous of her progress. She had earlier reported to the worker that her neighbors had isolated her, encouraging their children not to play with her children, and even had attempted to halt her effort at becoming drug free by putting a package (with drugs) in her mailbox. The package was labeled: "This is for you." In a similar fashion she was ambivalent about changing and the losses it would entail. Thus when Lena was first approached to assume the paid group leader role, she had responded doubtfully: "I don't feel strong enough." Even with support from the worker, three months after deciding to assume this role, she asked to "give it up and let others volunteer." Still unready, she needed more help to manage the losses, conflict, and rivalry with her neighbors.

For Lena, growing accustomed to success and competency in leadership took some time. Recognizing this as a need for other group members as well as Lena, the agency brought in a speaker on community leadership. Members responded with interest, raising questions about their changing roles in empowering their own lives, their families, and communities. In this connection another goal for the group involved learning about victimization and oppression, and finding ways to deal with and overcome the debilitating impact of these forces on individuals and the neighborhood.

For example, on occasion the practitioner directed discussion to the way in which the social system influenced the women's relationships with their men, how it emasculated the men and then blamed them for their responses. When the women raised the issue about their companions' frustrations regarding the lack of jobs, she reinforced ideas suggesting how group members could become supportive of the men, helping them to grow rather than simply putting them out and cutting them off, and later taking them back. The idea was to interrupt the vicious cycle whereby men circulate from woman to woman and back to mother, making a permanent connection with no one (except mother).

The Men in the Lives of Lena, Tanya, and Della

While these mothers were finding assistance in a support group, their boyfriends and husbands refused agency overtures to organize a group for men. Although they did allow themselves to be involved in couple and family sessions, albeit reluctantly, they often came late, participated minimally, became embroiled in conflict, or missed sessions. When on occasion they attended the drug awareness group, their participation was uneven—sometimes even confrontational and sometimes uninvolved.

The problems of these men seemed to stem from their inadequate sense of connection and belonging. They appeared less ready to open up and bond, to accept mutual aid responsibilities, to work toward democratic, shared governance goals, and to engage in the hard tasks of problem solving. Seemingly unable to see or receive benefit from connecting to others, they preferred to remain autonomous and uncommitted either to relationships in the group or to the dynamics that mark group process. Their lack of clear personal goals, their exploitative behaviors, their lack of employment as well as nonemployability added to the systemic forces entrapping them, their women, and their offspring.[20]

A major issue that compromises group and individual work with men is the "norm of distrust,"[21] borne of their earlier experiences with powerlessness in the community, particularly at the hands of authority figures including those in law enforcement. While such distrust is often laid at the doorstep of family functioning and parenting, particularly mothering, insufficient attention is given to these other non-maternal or familial, perhaps more significant, sources in their lives. Having spent much time on the streets, with limited access to positive role models, they have learned the unattractive side of those who were available. Such experiences as being shaken down by a cop and having their earnings from illegal drug activity taken and pocketed and being informed that they'll "be let off this time" makes a lasting impression. What behaviors will they imitate or model? What have they been taught about values and ethics when the only employed adult males they know get illegal as well as legal payoffs?

This norm of distrust, which has become an adaptation to power-lessness for too many in this population, often extracts a heavy price from practitioners: enormous effort and energy are required to reach each client, and much additional time is needed for outreach and transcending the protective wall that clients erect if the comfort zone needed for meaningful engagement and successful intervention outcome is to be reached. The extensive effort needed can be undermined if practitioners are not in control of their own personal power needs and are unable to engage in the one-down behavior or demonstration of vulnerability that is sometimes necessary. In fact a sense of entitlement of any kind on the part of the practitioner (whether it stems from personal power need, perception of self as expert, or from high cultural group status assignment—for example, being white, upper middle class, or male) will compromise the endeavor. Practitioners must have the capacity to manage their entitled expectations and not be turned off when such clients resist them by showing coolness, aloofness, and playing hard to get. A seasoned consultant reports that his first advice to practitioners working with youth and young adults (particularly males) from such populations is to avoid at all costs getting into a power game, backing them into a corner: a sure recipe for trouble. Having felt put down and devalued all their lives, they will not tolerate what they perceive as being "dissed" (disrespected) by anyone, including a practitioner. Those who are familiar with their relationship and behavioral style describe the protective wall that surrounds them. A seasoned practitioner commented:

> When a youth has *no* self-esteem, when there is nothing to build on— watch him. He will take you out in a second.

It is well to remember that the attraction of the gang group, an adaptive strategy discussed in more detail in Chapter 7, is that it provides a haven from abandonment, a source of security, both financial and emotional, and a base of respect for kids who lack these. The young boy mentioned earlier who participated in the agency's youth activities and stated that he was "scared" was seeking refuge from a gang that was recruiting heavily.

Coming from similar childhood experiences, the boyfriends and husbands of Lena, Tanya, and Della experienced such distrust. Along with many others, they had rarely felt valued and respected and in turn showed little respect for their women, children, neighborhood, and helping agencies.

Parenthetically, the authors are mindful of how little practitioners knew about the men in contrast to the women, including not knowing all of their full names. The profound sense of disconnection experienced by these men and their alienation from help and support were noted earlier. More fundamentally, perhaps it is another example of the nullification of the black male in American society.[22]

The information highway open to males in this population constitutes yet another issue related to their isolation and entrapment. Blocked from access to systems unless through formal channels, men on the street corner know there are few groups they can join that can provide informal access to information about jobs, educational programs, or better housing. The informal systems that work well for them tend to be ones that dispense information regarding drugs, running games, and other exploitative activities involving both self and community. Effective practitioners, group workers, and community organizers know that there is a needful population that could be engaged if resources were available for serious individual, group, and community development. We share some successful group work with seriously overwhelmed men in Chapters 4, 6, and 7.

3

GROUP FORMATION AND DEVELOPMENT

Women Moving Forward Group;
Parenting Group for Recovering Addict Mothers

PURPOSE OF GROUPS

The purpose of groups in the context of this discussion may be stated as leveraging individual attributes and strengths to facilitate personal and collective empowerment.[1] For example, the Women Moving Forward group served as a mediating force and a mutual support system[2] for its members, providing a mechanism for managing and changing dysfunctional behaviors. In her battle to remain drug free, the group offered Lena some reality-based control, raising as it did questions about who would care for her children and whether her children needed her, and supplying friendship to fill the void she experienced in moving away from her drug-addicted friends. Such a peer support approach capitalizes on the gratification experienced by people when they believe they can benefit and become empowered by the group experience.

Such an experience is created when the group provides supports for day-to-day survival (reinforcements for staying away from drugs; for avoiding destructive, seductive romantic relationships; for organizing parenting routines that facilitate prompt school attendance by children and prompt work attendance); for accentuating positive attributes (sharing information on improving one's personal presentation; for enhancing coping skills, expanding negotiation skills, developing anger management techniques); and for improving one's basic knowledge (by learning to read, learning to use help, to seek interpretations of policies and procedures). Processing these activities with the help of others facilitates a sense of empowerment and positive change that translates into a better quality of life for these women and their families. Such growth and development of members was clearly observed in the Women Moving Forward group as they worked to reach individual and group goals.

RECRUITING AND SCREENING MEMBERS

Successful group outcome depends on careful attention to every phase of group development. The complexities involved in group formation are often underestimated and minimized. Targeting and screening of members, the first stage to be discussed here, requires thorough assessment of the fit between potential members and the composition and purpose of the group. How the group should be composed demands consideration of such issues as optimal size of group and of member characteristics such as age, ethnicity, race, gender, and class. Once decisions have been made by the practitioner regarding these variables, recruitment and screening can begin. Again the Women Moving Forward group is instructive. Here the practitioner engaged in aggressive outreach by approaching mothers through their interest in their children's group experience. On or near the playground at the agency and in other neighborhood sites where mothers were involved with their children, they were approached regarding possible interest in a group experience of their own. Outreach was facilitated by the agency's knowledge of the families and by extensive contacts and activities with the children.

Another recruitment approach, announcing the formation of the group, was employed for the Parenting Group for Recovering Addict Mothers. Referrals were sought from agency and hospital-based practi-

tioners as well as from successful clients, that is, those who had benefited from the group experience. Contacting these potential members
via phone and discussing the possibility of involvement in the group
enabled the practitioner to make some early judgments about each individual and the degree to which there would be a good fit with the
group. This initial discussion was guided by a brief list of questions
that assessed need for the experience, interest and motivation, readiness for participation, and clarity about group purpose. Prospective
members' clarity on the purpose of the group—for example, providing
support for recovering addicts, providing training for recovering addict
mothers—was essential to avoid confusion, misunderstanding, and
vagueness about the intended experience. Other concerns such as
members' ability to attend regularly and what fees would be required
were also addressed in this early dialogue between practitioner and potential member.

After the phone contact a personal conference was arranged. This
face-to-face meeting allowed the worker to make a stronger assessment
regarding client suitability for the group and also to process the issue of
agency and client expectations related to the group experience. What
did the client, as potential member, expect to achieve? What concerns
and expectations were held by the clients? Housekeeping details, such
as fees for group activities, transportation (especially for evening sessions), attendance, and promptness, were clarified. Clients wished to
know "who else" would join the group. Racial and ethnic concerns
may be discussed here also, especially if the composition of a group will
be diverse.

In the Parenting Group for Recovering Addict Mothers, the practitioner interviewed each potential member, looking for common goals
and facilitative personal characteristics including interest, stamina,
and capacity for sharing and growth. Some hostile, destructive, narcissistic persons did not appear ready for the demands of the group
process and thus were not referred. This is a judgment call by the practitioner. Persons who were deemed not serious about giving up drugs
were screened out, as were clients suffering from severe emotional impairment which could result in communication and relationship prob-

lems within the group. For such persons a group experience with a focus on socialization skills might be more appropriate. A mother who was still doing drugs, and whose presence might be disruptive given her vulnerability to impulsive behavior when under the influence, would be seen as better served by a drug treatment group. The accuracy of the practitioner's judgment about suitability is key.

A practitioner working with another mothers' drug recovery group had earlier permitted a client suspected of still being on drugs to participate. Not aware of the extent of this client's dependency, she was startled to learn from members of another group she was leading about this former client's death from a drug overdose. All group members were challenged by this news. Death and loss, instead of child management and parenting concerns, became the focus of the group. The practitioner, troubled about her misassessment of the gravity of this client's problem, and burdened with her own responses of guilt, anger, and slackness, doubted her own competence and faced some personal stress as a result of the tragedy. Later she reflected, "I hated to lose her—I wanted so much to help her."

Many group members as well as the practitioner were concerned with questions about the care and future of this client's children, who had already been placed with relatives by the state department of social services. Some members acknowledged that if they had not "gotten straight" they too might have overdosed and wondered, "What would have happened to my kids? Who would take care of them?"

Such questions certainly sobered members and at the same time helped to give them new insights about the needs of their children and the value of being competent, caring mothers.

CONTRACTING FOR INDIVIDUAL GROUP GOALS AND OUTCOMES

Once motivation becomes clear and expectations are clarified, practitioner and prospective members can engage in more formal agreement concerning the group experience. Encouraging a client to establish individual goals is necessary since these will serve as a useful guide for monitoring personal change and identifying movement toward higher functioning. The activity scope is to help clients set doable goals that will be consistent with the overall purpose of the future group. In the Women Moving Forward group, individual members targeted goals that, once formed, enhanced the growth and movement of the group. Individual goals included improvement in:

- Personal skills
- Parenting skills
- Reading skills

The practitioner, as prospective leader, helped clarify agency and prospective members' expectations concerning a number of issues:

Behavior

- Regular attendance
- Promptness
- Not bringing friends/guests without approval
- Personal (do not come if you are high and spaced out)
- Participation—ability to open up and self-disclose
- Speaking with respect, expressing thoughts and perspective without fear of retaliation
- No profanity

Values

- Democratic orientation
- Respect for each member
- Nondiscrimination
- Confidentiality and privacy
- Appropriate social relationships

Clarifying behavioral expectations and values at the outset lays the basis for the group's establishment of procedures. Facilitating smoother, less conflictual interactions, such a structure serves key purposes, including individual control and management of interaction styles among and between members. An expectation that members will speak with respect for one another, for example, helps to insure that all views can be expressed despite differences of opinion and even occasional conflict. Acquiring the capacity to tolerate differences of opinion and action is indicative of growth.

Agency Responsibility

The practitioner reviewed with each prospective member what she expected of the agency:

- Provision of hospitable, comfortable, private space
- Provision of safe space for records
- Respect for privacy and confidentiality

Practitioner Expectations

Also reviewed were the expectations of the practitioner which included:

- Democratic approach to leadership
- Respect for clients
- Nondiscrimination
- Review of practitioner's role as group leader
- When practitioner should intervene to facilitate discussion
- When practitioner should intervene to block conflict or protect confidentiality

Group Size

Optimum group size is highly influenced by group purpose. For example, supportive growth-oriented groups are usually smaller then task-oriented groups. Size influences many key dynamics of a group such as opportunity to develop and exercise leadership which is in turn influenced by structure of communication and range of members' participation. Communication structure is defined as "who speaks to whom about what and under what circumstances."[3] Again, the Women Moving Forward group is illustrative. Its size of three to six members permitted open discussion, disclosure, sharing, and participation in the type of activities that facilitated personal growth. In contrast, a task-oriented, open-ended neighborhood improvement group with sixteen members, being much larger, did not offer members the personal space needed for extensive disclosure.

The comfort level of prospective members with the size of the group was also a consideration. Some individuals are uncomfortable dealing with more than a few people. To others, a large group is welcome, providing a potential forum or stage. If at all possible these highly personal concerns are reviewed and negotiated prior to the first group session.

Logistics: Announcement of Meeting, Location of Session, Time, and Other

In the Parenting Group for Recovering Addict Mothers, announcement of the first group session was sent to all potential members indicating time, location and address of agency, room number at the agency, and phone number of practitioner in the event there were last-minute questions or concerns. The announcements were very attractive, in bright color, and often in multiple languages—English, Spanish, and French. The following concerns were manifested:

"My baby sitter hasn't gotten here—Can I bring my baby with me?"

"I can't do it today, I don't feel up to it."

"I want to come but my boyfriend don't want me to come."

The practitioner, prepared for response to a number of situations and calls for help, talked members through their fears and crises.

THE FIRST GROUP SESSION

Coming together for the first session is a time of both anxiety and anticipation. What is it really going to be like? Who am I going to meet? What will others think about me? Will they like me? Anxiety stemming from fear of rejection and put-down is high in the overwhelmed population, owing to life experience in a society they view as punitive and in which there are few, if any, moderating influences to change that view. There is also, however, anticipation and hopefulness for some positive benefit—someone to care about them, someone to understand what a struggle it has been to give up drugs, and someone to share the joy of regaining custody of their children.

When members arrived at the agency they were warmly greeted. Receptionists, alerted by the practitioner that members would be arriving at a scheduled time, met them at the door, directing or escorting them to the meeting room where coffee and tea were offered. As one practitioner who worked with this population expressed it: "We must treat our clients as valued guests in our home."

After an exchange of pleasantries over coffee, those who had gathered were invited to begin the group process; typically, chairs were arranged in a circle. The practitioner gave her name and a bit of information about her experience running groups. In the Parenting Group for Recovering Addict Mothers, those who attended for the first session introduced themselves:

Jane: 31 years old, mother of three, drug addict for six years, in recovery for one year.

Clara: Single mother of two children in state custody. Sober for six months.

Ed: Mother of four children who were soon to be returned to her. Sober for six months from cocaine and alcohol.

Racquel: Mother of three children in the custody of a relative. Wanted to get her children back.

Elizabeth (Betty): A grandmother caring for an adult daughter's child and her own young son.

Marla: 25-year-old mother of one child, recovering from cocaine abuse.

Tashika: Recovering from multidrug abuse, but mainly cocaine. Caring for her sister's children, a boy and a girl.

Ora: Mother of five children all in custody of state. Struggling with alcoholism.

Evelyn: Mother of three children in her mother's custody.

Wilma: Pregnant mother of two children.

Rita: Single mother of four children; oldest two now residing with their father, third child with her father's mother, fourth with Rita and her partner who is baby's father. Struggled with cocaine. Wants the three children back.

Members explained why they had come; that is, they discussed personal goals that had been noted previously in the telephone conferences and personal interviews. A majority of the mothers in the group, having lost custody of their children due to abuse and/or neglect, expressed earnest wishes to have their children returned to them. Becoming better mothers and being able to raise their children without outside interference were important goals. All of the members, as recovering addicts, stated their intention to remain free of alcohol/drug addiction, which they well understood was key to keeping their children. After these initial greetings and introductions, the practitioner moved quickly to help focus on rules for the group, goals, and a working agenda.

Manifest and Latent Rules, Guides, and Norms

The pregroup discussion between the practitioner and prospective members concerning behavioral and value expectations served as a basis for the group's early consideration of rules and guides. This discussion was held to facilitate a collective establishment of expectations for appropriate behaviors. For example, addressing members with respect had been suggested by the practitioner as an expectation. Now the group could agree that indeed each member would be addressed and responded to with respect. Another area of agreement dealt with the confidential nature of the material shared in group sessions. It was decided that what each member revealed "would not leave the room." Regardless of the nature of the problem and the pain that surfaced, members were not to speak about such to anyone, including their friends, spouses, siblings, or neighbors. The risks involved in sharing that exist for recovering addicts were clarified since some were in different phases of their struggles to remain sober, to get their children back, and/or to maintain financial support from some form of public assistance. Yet another expectation of all participants was that of shared responsibility for the group's progress.

These general guides or rules facilitated participation, encouraging members to start out being open, respectful, and up front with one another. In addition to these manifest guides/rules, there were also the latent ones that, while not articulated, were equally important. Among them was the expectation that members would support and encourage one another when needed, for example reaching out to a member in pain so that she would not be alone. Another was the recognition that, although all members shared responsibility for group participation, the capacity of each to communicate verbally differed from member to member and some could not open up as much—certainly not in the beginning. Though not explicit, these norms were nonetheless understood. In the parenting group, once guides were discussed and agreed upon, they were written down and handed out so that members could review them while away from the agency.

Throughout the life of the group, the practitioner helped members to open up, self-disclose, and maintain a readiness to examine their attitudes and behaviors and think about personal growth and positive change. In this way, cohesion and trust among members were facilitated.

Group Goals and Agenda Building

In the parenting group, which was more structured and directed than many groups, an outline was handed out to facilitate goal setting and agenda building. The topics included:

- Introductions/Parenting Experience
- Parenting Issues
- Cultural Diversity
- Self-Development (2 sessions)
- Video: Alternatives to Spanking (2 sessions)
- Managing Discipline/Gaining Cooperation
- Self-Esteem in Children
- Sexuality in Children
- Summary/Evaluation

Women Moving Forward was less structured than the parenting group and did not have a designated time limit. In the latter, members' battles with drugs and alcohol was a recurrent issue as every ounce of personal resolve was needed to mobilize the necessary motivation and stamina. Members helped one another in this struggle by providing support and encouragement, sending reminders to "hang in there, sister" and to look for positives in their lives.

Group goals emerged from the common interests, needs, and aspirations of all parties—members, practitioner, and agency—that were embodied in the discussions. The process involves the pursuit of several goals which exist simultaneously and are addressed both by members and the practitioner.[4] For both the Women Moving Forward group and the parenting group, goals included the following:

- Mutual aid
- Support and empathy
- Information sharing
- Education
- Parenting knowledge and skills

Within the two groups emphasis clearly differed but similar threads surfaced in the sessions, reflecting the appropriate pursuit of different group purposes. Remember, Women Moving Forward was started to support their children's activities, and while members had a variety of concrete problems they did not perceive themselves as seriously depleted by psychological and drug problems. In the Parenting Group for Recovering Addict Mothers all members had major substance abuse problems as a result of which most had lost custody of their children and one member later lost her life. Also drugs and alcohol had dictated how most if not all of their economic resources were being used. In both groups a number of the women, enmeshed in abusive, exploitative relationships, possessed no greater skill in dealing with abusive love—men—than in dealing with addictive love—drugs.

The Parenting Group for Recovering Addict Mothers was a structured, short-term group composed of eleven members, five of whom came regularly. All were struggling in recovery from substance abuse. Seven of them—Clara, Ed, Racquel, Ora, Evelyn, Jane, and Rita—had lost custody of their children. One member had recently secured the return of her children; three others were caring for their own children. One of these was a grandmother who was also caring for her adult daughter's child and another was an aunt caring for a niece and nephew. Both were also recovering addicts. All of the five regular members had received lengthy treatment.

Tashika, who had received help for her lengthy addiction to cocaine and several other drugs, entered the group with a firm goal to get her life "back on track." She was highly invested in parenting, having now become the caretaker of her niece and nephew. She was seeking help in setting the correct limits and what would be most beneficial to the children. In discussing her growing-up experiences with her own parents and her experiences in parenting her niece and nephew, her sadness was often noted by group members, who would extend comfort. Tashika was also able to offer comfort to others.

Betty, who served as mother figure for the group, was the only member who took responsibility for her addiction, declaring, "My family brought me up properly and my cocaine use is solely my responsibility: it's my own fault." She had ended an abusive relationship with her partner and was currently living in a stable situation.

Betty, a grandmother caring for her adult daughter's child and her own young son, was struggling to keep her family intact. In the group, she was very supportive of other members who looked to her for advice. She would take risks by "speaking my mind," later having to deal with the consequences. Despite her strong presentation, Betty was also very vulnerable as demonstrated by her behavior when she was describing incidents that caused her personal pain.

Marla, a young mother of a three-year-old, was a recovering cocaine abuser. Her son, who had been in her mother's care for a brief time, was now back in her custody. She was enmeshed in relational issues with a boyfriend, and the group offered ideas, suggestions, and support on how to manage the relationship. Marla also expressed need for "help with limit setting" with her son and found very useful the parenting guidelines offered by the leader and also group members' suggestions about ways to apply them. In the discussions, Marla was vibrant and energetic with a ready smile and a positive response to the pain which some members expressed in relation to their problems.

Jane, a cocaine addict for six years who was now in recovery for one year, had three children: one in her care, one in foster care, and one with a relative. Currently, Jane attended a day treatment program three times per week. Her goal was to get her children back, and she had worked hard to change her behavior. However, she was experiencing a great deal *of difficulty because the state did not concur that she had completed all of the requirements of the service plan. In the sessions, it was not uncommon for her to try to dominate discussion with concerns about her own needs and desire to get her two children back. Members became impatient with her, though they did not voice this sentiment. As time went on, they were able to help Jane understand that she wasn't ready to have her children back; they said directly that "it was not right for the children to go to you yet."*

Clara was a single mother of two children who were in custody of the state. Now sober for six months, she had been in treatment at several detox programs. In the sessions, Clara revealed a pleasant attitude and strong determination to get her children back. Clara was supportive of other members and shared willingly her own struggles but would not usually challenge others if she disagreed with them. In these exchanges, more assertive members would extend support to Clara, helping her to clarify her ideas and make her views known.

Rita was a 35-year-old stunningly beautiful mother of four, who looked like a model. Living with her current partner, she was caring for only one of her children, the youngest. The two older children were with their father; another child was also with her father and actually being cared for by his mother. Three fathers were involved with Rita and the four children.

Rita, an only child, succumbed to drugs early on, having seen her mother abusing substances. Despite her addiction, Rita's mother always dressed attractively; looking good and drugging up were traits mother and daughter shared.

In the group, Rita expressed how much she wanted her children back. She expected the group to agree with her opinion of the department of social services when she described how her custody issues were handled; however, this did not usually happen. Often dominating the discussion, Rita would also ask questions, seemingly seeking help, but could not wait for answers.

In the early sessions individual problems and needs became clear, as did the goals of members who were regular in their participation. Some members were less successful than others, and some were unable to benefit much from the group. They dropped out after the first one or two sessions or attended the remaining sessions sporadically.

> *Ora, for example, came to only one session. Now in alcohol recovery, she was a depressed, obese mother of five children who were all in custody of the state. She was apprehensive about the group, initially withholding and reluctant to share. As the session progressed she became less hesitant but remained skeptical. At the end of her first meeting there was clearly a question whether she would return; she did not.*
>
> *Evelyn made it through three sessions. Mother of three children who were in her mother's custody, she had visitation rights but did not always follow through. In sharing feelings and commenting on questions and issues, Evelyn appeared to have sound knowledge and clear thinking. Yet there was a sense that she doubted whether she could gain much from the group; her motivation and commitment to the process never seemed strong.*
>
> *Wilma and Ed, who also dropped out, experienced problems not unlike Ora and Evelyn. They were unable to fully engage and confront personal problems in the manner needed to set individual goals and commit to group goals. One member who dropped out said that she felt "overwhelmed at times by all that I have to overcome." Obviously she did not view the group as a helping resource but rather as one more demand.*
>
> *Another member, Racquel, who had attended sporadically four of the ten sessions, had overdosed two months after termination of the group. Of note was the fact that the sessions she missed were those focusing on self-development and self-care. During a discussion on sexual abuse she had reacted very strongly, stating: "When I was younger and attractive I could get any man I wanted. Now look at me, look at me. I don't look good as I used to."*
>
> *After the session Racquel showed more serious symptoms of depression; later that day she had to be hospitalized. Clinicians at the agency played a major role in helping arrange the needed medical attention.*

The members of this group were all African-American, except for Racquel, who was a Latina. The practitioner realized that as the only culturally different member she might well experience stress related to feeling isolated and perceiving a lack of commonalty between her background and the others. A similar group composed primarily of African-Americans contained one member who was white but in the initial interview with the practitioner had identified herself as black and requested admission to the group. This mother of two children, one biracial and one white, had dropped out early in the group experience after members discussed their experiences and relationships with whites in a manner she processed as negative. Skillful though the practitioner was, she was unable to prevent the member from experiencing isolation and rejection.

In vulnerable, frail populations diversity often compounds the many dynamics that operate, retarding or even preventing bonding and the affiliation needed to accomplish group goals. Though not discriminatory, many of these groups end up being ethnically homogeneous.

What has been shown so far in this discussion of goals and agenda setting is the connection and interrelationship between individual/member goals (e.g., staying sober, getting kids back, becoming a better mom) and the main goal of the group (e.g., helping recovering addicts improve their capacity for parenting). Goal clarity, for both individual members and the group, helps facilitate movement to desired outcomes.[5]

Group Process: Roles, Leadership, and Power in the Beginning Phase

Even in the beginning phase of the Parenting Group for Recovering Addict Mothers some of the relationship patterns[6] became evident. Different members assumed particular roles, some becoming friends both in and out of the group setting; others taking on leadership roles, helping the group to completion of instrumental tasks, and still others dominating discussion, having to have the "last word," insisting that their particular view "is right."

Betty, as noted earlier, was caring for her adult daughter's child and her own son. She was the only member who was able to accept full responsibility for her addiction. She declared: "I did it. I know my daughter became an addict because of what I did. I used drugs in front of her."

The pain was evident in her voice, on her face, and in the tension in her body. In the first two sessions, when members moved off track, she would help direct the group back to the subject of parenting. It was not unusual for her to say "Let's deal with what we did as the parent." Others, Tashika, Marla, and Clara, but especially Marla, would also help reinforce that, as parents, they all had particular responsibilities for their children's plight as well as their future.

Marla wanted help with limit setting for her three-year-old son, Jon, and also requested assistance with relational issues with her partner. She said, "I don't know what to do about my son. He acts up and I give in to him."

Betty responded:

> "Don't always give in to him. Don't reward him for acting up. Jon should not always get what he wants. You don't have to give him what he wants just because he wants something."

Betty, Clara, and others observed that perhaps Marla was feeling guilty about her past drugging behavior which had resulted in her losing custody of Jon. They wondered whether, now that they were together, this guilt made it hard for her to set necessary and important limits. During these exchanges, Clara became especially supportive of Marla and the two often talked after group sessions over the phone, even getting together at home to help one another through crises.

Marla's growth was manifest in her increasing attractiveness and self-confidence; she was directive and helpful to others but in a manner that was less verbal than Betty. A quiet, positive influence, her warmth and easy smile helped reduce tension in the group.

Although Rita always received the group's attention when she spoke, she could never say enough. She talked and talked, blaming her mom for her addiction, social workers for taking her kids, boyfriends for messing up her life. She failed to take personal responsibility for any of these events, deeply traumatic as they were. In an early session she declared, "I want my kids back. I am sober." Betty, Marla, and Clara raised the following questions or concerns in the discussion that followed.

Betty asked, "Are you thinking about what is right for your kids?"
Marla added, "What do your kids think? What you gonna do about
your boyfriend? Where is he going to be?" Clara nodded agreement with
Marla. Rita declared over and over: "These are my kids. They are
mine."

Unable to "hear" and understand the group's concern about her
readiness to become a mother to the children, Rita became angry. She accused the group of turning on her and siding with the department of social services.

Rita was also embroiled in an intense struggle with the grandmother
of one of her children, a four-year-old girl. Betty, Marla, and Clara were
deeply concerned about how this child, who had been raised since birth
by her paternal grandmother, would feel about leaving her to return to
Rita. Clara, who was not usually assertive in making her views known,
asked, "Is she ready to leave her grandmother? Will she [grandmother] let
her go?" Several wondered if the child knew Rita, who responded with
entitlement to this question: "I'm her ma. I have a right to my kids. She
[grandmother] can't keep me from my girl." This child, who had become
particularly attached to her grandmother, had expressed reluctance and
fear about leaving to join Rita, her baby, and her partner in a new
home. The women were able to empathize with the child and echoed
Betty's advice to Rita: "Slow it down, stop and think. It's not just you and
what you want. Think about your child."

Rita repeatedly complained, "DSS took my kids," and "My own
mother didn't help. She could have taken my kids or at least helped me
more." It was Betty who initially helped focus on the reality by saying,
"You lost your own kids because you used drugs. You couldn't manage
your kids."

Rita became increasingly agitated, dominating the discussion and
continuing to blame her mom, DSS, and social workers. As feelings
heated up a bit and discomfort, even conflict, surfaced, Betty, Marla,
Clara, and Tashika encouraged Rita to "chill out." Marla smiled and
extended her hand and others offered similar support, but no one agreed
that she was ready to receive her children.

Jane, whose situation with DSS regarding progress on her service plan
was similar to Rita's, said, "I know it's hard. I know how hard it is."

Jane, too, often had harsh words for DSS, painfully expressing how she wanted her kids back but the social workers always blocked it with "No, not yet."

Later in the discussion it was revealed that Rita's mother was an addict. Upon learning this the women helped Rita understand how unrealistic she was to think that her mother was in a position to help her when, in fact, her mother needed treatment for drug abuse.

Helping Rita and, to a lesser extent, Jane focus on how their own behaviors helped get them into their difficult circumstances took up a good bit of the time in the early group sessions. Encouraging both Rita and Jane to stop blaming others and especially DSS, and helping Rita to stop scapegoating her mother and to accept personal responsibility required much energy and persistence. However, the group was a significant beginning step in the process of preparing them to become better parents. Other members benefited too.

Marla received tips on limit setting with Jon and struck up a friendship with Clara that proved very helpful. Their bond was particularly noticeable in the concern and support Clara offered when Marla reported the following upsetting incident: One day while Jon was playing in the yard outside his home, within hearing distance of Marla but out of her sight, a stranger came by and tried to abduct the boy. Jon's screams attracted Marla's attention and she, frightened, also screamed for help which frightened away the would-be abductor. Marla was very shaken by the incident and Clara's empathy, sitting with her and offering support, probably helped her avoid a retreat to drugs for escape.

Even in these early sessions certain members assumed important roles. Betty no doubt provided important leadership, aiding the group to focus on the hard task of parenting and not getting caught in scapegoating and victimization syndromes. Her thoughtful, timely insights also helped the group to become a more cohesive unit. Her up-front, clear comments were persuasive and conveyed a certain wisdom which influenced others. Marla too provided leadership, though not in a manner as directive as Betty's. Carla, not usually verbal, helped keep discussion moving by certain body language—nodding her head with an occasional positive "Yeah!" Although Evelyn also was positive, she couldn't stick with it, and dropped out of the group early. Rita presented herself as always in a struggle—with DSS, with one former boyfriend's mother in particular (who had been caring for one of Rita's children since birth), and with the group members. She tried to dominate the time with her own issue: "Getting my kids back. Period." Her need to be center stage, which she usually was anyway because of her beauty and style, spoke to great neediness.

When Rita was confronted with her tendency to scapegoat others and dominate discussion, were her power struggles reduced? Was she able to become more open in her thinking, processing information from members? From time to time, the practitioner had repeatedly directed the group to the topic of parenting per se, in keeping with the agenda. Reflecting on the group process, she noted "there were few power struggles in this group, though helping them stay focused was often challenging." This, the practitioner advised, had not been the case in another group, the Parenting Group for Recovering Addict Fathers, which will be discussed in Chapter 4. Of interest are emerging ideas on how gender-specific groups form, develop, and progress.

Group Process: Roles of Members in Middle Phase

As the group moved from the beginning into the middle phase focusing on members' self-development and parenting issues such as managing discipline, alternatives to spanking, and ways to gain cooperation from their children, the roles of members became even clearer, as did the capacity of members to stick with the group and confront pressing personal challenges. Though competitiveness and antagonism were managed and kept in balance by the practitioner, on a very few occasions such attitudes did surface. Betty continued to bring expertise by demonstrating ongoing acceptance of responsibility for her predicament and questioning how she might have lived her life differently. She declared: "I am going to see this out, stay off drugs, and get a job."

Her determination was uplifting and her self-esteem had increased, a manifestation of the benefit received from the members' support and the practitioner's reinforcement. Marla was also growing stronger and feeling more confident. She tested out strategies for limit setting with Jon on the group, receiving and apparently using their feedback with some success. Similarly, she was able to share information about her relationship with her partner and again feedback from her group sisters seemed useful. Marla was tested, however, when, now feeling much more competent and much stronger, she agreed to help her mother care for her brother who had been exploiting their mother: jobless and living in her home, he refused to contribute to expenses or the maintenance. The brother moved into Marla's apartment and continued such behavior. Marla reviewed her expectations after which she and her brother agreed that he would find a job and contribute a reasonable share toward living expenses; but he failed to follow up as bargained. Part of the understanding was that he would have to leave if he did not contribute, but he probably never expected Marla to take action on what was becoming an increasingly difficult and aggravating struggle and force him to leave.

Rita discussed her relationships with each of her four children and how she hoped to respond when she got her children back. We noted earlier her struggle with the grandmother of her four-year-old. Her oldest, a girl of ten years, presented a perplexing dilemma. She seemed more satisfied when Rita was drugging it up because of the lovely expensive gifts Rita bought her with the drug money. Rita explained, "My ten-year-old doesn't like it now because I can't get her what she wants." She received support from the group to help her cope with her "low times" and her frustration at not being able to give to her daughter. Betty reassured her, "You are now giving her what she needs—time with you." Others—Tashika, Marla, and Clara agreed—noting how she should replace jewelry and fancy clothes—which had always been important to the well-attired Rita—with time. They urged her to visit with her children more and talk with them. "Really talk, listen, read, and play with the children." Rita did try. After a few weeks of making more of an effort to be with her kids, DSS remained unconvinced that she was ready for reunification with her children and Rita became enraged. The group felt that she should work even harder to get the children back. Unable to accept the confrontation from members, their gentle but firm control, Rita dropped out a little more than halfway through the group experience.

Upon Rita's departure Jane moved to assume a very open and challenging role, not unlike that of Rita though she was slightly more open to receiving inputs on parenting. Highly invested, Tashika welcomed new ideas on parenting, and on her own self-development/improvement.

Self-development sessions were planned around questions that related to members' perceived strengths and weaknesses. In the first session they were given a questionnaire to take home and return the following week. Some responses included:

Strengths

- "I am a good person."
- "I am a good parent."
- "I am a fighter."
- "I can fight DSS for my children."

Weaknesses

- "I am not a good person."
- "I am not a good parent."
- "I can't take care of my own children."
- "I ain't able to care of myself or my kids."
- "I ain't got a job."
- "I'm homeless."

Usually members identified many more weaknesses than strengths. In reviewing their responses, however, the practitioner helped each to identify several more positives and encouraged other members to join in:

- "Rita, you are so attractive."
- "Clara is smart."
- "Tashika, you are real good. You're keeping your niece and nephew."

Positive energy flowed, mobilized by the practitioner's opening ritual, in which she encouraged them to "Breathe in strength, the beauty of the day; breathe out bad feelings; push out negative events, all the negative energy."

This quiet exercise encouraged members to focus on their own self-development and self-care, acknowledge their hard-won battles with drugs and progress on life goals, and attend to their most important goal: getting and/or keeping their children.

Toward the End

The five members who finished the group—Betty, Tashika, Marla, Clara, and Jane—became close, particularly Marla and Clara. While Marla was a strong member, Betty remained the key leader and also became a mother figure. Jane hung in there. Group members were delighted when Clara, who was never very verbal but who was obviously involved, gave evidence that she was actively processing the content of the meeting. When she was reunited with her children, the group celebrated the good news.

Marla, who struggled with limit setting with Jon while continuing to generate warmth and openness, became more self-confident. She had struggled with her brother, who refused to follow through and get a job. With support from her group sisters, she put her brother out, although the pain of seeing him on the streets with no job and no home was exceedingly difficult. Marla also got rid of her partner. Now she was seeing a brighter future for herself and was preparing to attend the local community college.

Tashika, quiet but strong, enjoyed sobriety and the companionship of her sister's children, whose thriving was so important to her. She was facing the challenge of helping her sister see the need for drug treatment.

Betty got a job and began using her obvious talent and skills to help others face their drugging habits and take the first step toward treatment. She was a featured speaker in one agency's drug awareness/prevention program. The big plus was that she helped her own drugging daughter to obtain sobriety. However the daughter was not yet able to care for her child and Betty continued to keep her grandchild.

Jane made progress, stopped much of her usual scapegoating, and was closer to reunification with her children, visiting regularly with them, their social worker, and the DSS social worker.

Rita returned to the group on the last day when all received certificates. She displayed her usual behavior: putting down her mother and scapegoating DSS and the grandmother of one of her children in particular. After that final group session, she came to the agency for a conference on the status of her reunification request. Upon hearing a negative response from DSS, she had a major outburst, swearing at the social worker and calling her every "mother what" you might imagine. Two practitioners who had not worked with Rita but who had seen her often and who had exchanged pleasantries with her in the past went to help her. Though it took immense effort and time, they were able to get Rita to calm herself down and talk about issues and next steps. Rita learned the painful lesson that earning a certificate for completion of the parenting group would require hard personal work. Maybe she would now start with another group.

The size of the group, five regularly attending members, was such that all had ample opportunity to express themselves and participate fully, though the capacity for participation certainly differed among members. Those who "hung in" were able to develop cohesion, trust, and a comfortable style of communication, and they worked toward growth in an environment of security which resulted in accomplishment of many individual and group goals. Goal attainment was no doubt facilitated by the inability of several others to maintain membership, thereby reducing tensions that can often be generated by less focused or determined members. Opportunities for leadership were evident, although one member, Betty, embraced this role more than others.

PRACTITIONER ROLE

To help facilitate growth—to do good—and certainly to do no harm are the essence of the practitioner's role.

In work with overwhelmed clients, the provision of instruction and support is key, and this was certainly the case with the Women Moving Forward group: the practitioner contracted with prospective members in their individual pregroup interview that they should call her any time they felt they were "slipping back" on alcohol or drugs. In offering this support, it would have been inappropriate and unethical for the practitioner to discuss personal confidential matters in the group sessions. To avoid having such a dual role with group members, some agencies with sufficient resources would probably not allow a group practitioner to work on an individual basis with members of the group. However, this is a resource issue that often cannot be resolved ideally.

In the Women Moving Forward group, the practitioner also used an educative role in discussion with the women about their men, pointing out how noxious environmental conditions and deficits played a role in pushing them into many of their dysfunctional behaviors and showing how the women could help by understanding their men's plight and encouraging them to seek assistance (from the agency or health center) or enroll in school or training. She supported the members' consideration of how to break the cycle of putting the men out—and then taking them back later. She encouraged them to try to understand the meaning of their actions—for themselves and their offspring. Their hopes and aspired-to lifestyles were carefully examined, and several very different scenarios were created. In the end the women experienced less anger, fear, and confusion, and acquired a greater sense of mastery over their behavior with their men, becoming readier to stop the blaming syndrome and to begin helping the men to see the need for help.

In the several groups reviewed in this study, the practitioner's role was more active early on because of the need to respond affirmatively to pressing personal and environmental needs. Responding to client need that is exacerbated by punitive national policies, fiscal constraints, or other barriers to help requires immediate intervention in a manner that promises success within a short time frame. The practitioner was very knowledgeable about concrete resource needs of clients and gave valuable guidance outside the group on possible forms of assistance: how to get access to a particular government office in order to receive emergency aid, where to direct a relative or friend for aid with substance abuse, or what pantries would provide food. In the Parenting Group for Recovering Addict Mothers the practitioner was directive, keeping the members focused on the agenda, which was largely preset. Contracting in relation to the guides, rules, and norms was also specific and heavily, though not totally, influenced by the practitioner.

The time frame within which movement can be expected to occur in groups of middle-class, fee-for-service clients is different than that for most overwhelmed clients, particularly now that agencies and practitioners are being forced to work with limited resources while at the same time they must attend to and hopefully resolve many resulting crises. It is mandatory that practitioners respond assertively to clients' pressing personal problems. A drugging mom preparing for the return of beloved children who are now in state-assigned custody probably mobilizes a different sense of urgency for a practitioner than the mom who needs help with basic parenting. Practitioners and agencies who work with overwhelmed clients must be cognizant of the need to have supportive services available to members after the group has terminated. This differs from traditional practice where termination and the reliance on termination are used to develop new internal mechanisms for dealing with loss. Overwhelmed clients often without other communal or financial resources need to be able to return to the agency for the safe haven they may desperately need. An example is the way the agency and staff provided pivotal support for Rita when she learned that the department of social services would not permit reunification with her children. The point is that overwhelmed clients will come back, and not leaving the door open would represent another example of rejection.

It is probably obvious that in addition to knowledge of group process practitioners should develop some understanding of the changes in human physiology and behavior that are brought on by drug addiction. Reflecting on her experience, one practitioner commented:

> Drugs change people. They think and act differently. Thought processes are often altered. You would not believe how drugs make clients think and act. Some of the behavior is unreal.

Leadership and Power

In both Women Moving Forward and the Parenting Group for Recovering Addict Mothers, the practitioners' exercise of leadership and appropriate use of power are undeniable and inseparable.[7] Without their initiative, the groups may not have convened in the first place. Both practitioners played key roles in targeting, recruiting, and screening members, and continuously assessing and re-assessing members' potential for growth and change through the group experience. In the early sessions, members looked to the practitioners for explanations about the purpose of the group, what they might accomplish individually through a shared experience, and what the group might accomplish as a collective of individuals.

In the Parenting Group for Recovering Addict Mothers, the goals, agenda, and guides/norms were heavily influenced by the practitioner to whom members looked for expert guidance. Recognizing her position of leadership, and the power inherent in that role, the practitioner commented, "I give them all I know, from my experience of running groups on parenting for recovering addicts."

Acknowledging her own expertise and the power attributed to her by members she added:

> I look for strengths and try to see the positives that members bring. I work to bring out the best. All of the clients want to become better parents. I try to help them achieve their own goals through the group. I think I have been successful—the word is out and there are always people [recovering addicts] who seem to want to join.

How active and directive the practitioner must be in exerting leadership is to some extent determined by the health and capabilities of the members.[8] Although all of these recovering addict parents were poor people of color,[9] carrying heavy psychological and physiological burdens, the practitioner showed deep respect for them individually and collectively and shared her influence early on. For example, in introducing the agenda, she asked, "What do you think about the agenda that I am suggesting? It has worked out well with other groups but we can modify it now or as we move on."

Initially communication occurred primarily between members and the practitioner, but this gradually changed. As the group itself moved through the different development phases and as members opened up and shared experiences, interaction among them increased, a process that was carefully monitored and facilitated by the practitioner. Members soon were calling one another by name and asking one another for clarification of problems. "Marla, what is it that Jon does that you cannot handle?" asked Betty.

When Marla did not respond quickly, the practitioner urged her to take her time and think about her situation. Assisting Marla to respond to Betty thus reinforced member-to-member communication.

Betty's movement into a leadership role and the active roles assumed by Tashika and Marla were facilitated by the way in which the practitioner was able to share her power. Her commitment to democratic approaches in her leadership—encouraging participation of members—was demonstrated in her respect for their suggestions regarding additional themes for discussion and her encouragement of an open style of communication where all were included and listened to with respect. Members were reminded frequently that sharing experiences, trading insights, and supporting one another through the process could bring them at least a measure of growth, change, and hope.

The practitioner leveled with members, especially in the beginning phase but also throughout the group, explaining that "what one gets out of the group is determined in large measure by what one puts in." She told them, "It's your turn to tell your story."

This was her way of communicating that effective outcome is based on hard work. She herself was prepared for that work and ready to hold out high expectations for members. For example, in the context of the discussion the practitioner would ask for their assessment of how the group was going, of how they were relating to one another; whether any member felt she was not being listened to. In this dialogue, the practitioner focused on the process of the group experience as well as on the specific topic under discussion.

For some practitioners stepping back and giving up a very direct leadership/power role can be difficult.[10] Betty's previous experience in a group is an example. Her vulnerability, usually hidden behind her presentation of strength and containment, was revealed in her description of an incident that had occurred several months prior to her joining the parenting group. She, and other members of the previous group, had resisted the leader's effort to close off discussion of a particular topic which they considered important. Referring to the ground rules, namely that the group had final say about an agenda topic arrived at through exercise of democratic give and take,[11] Betty questioned the practitioner's insistence on ending the discussion and moving ahead, a sentiment echoed strongly by others.

Unable to tolerate this challenge to his position the practitioner had responded autocratically, asserting, "This is my group. You do what I tell you. I decide what we talk about." Later, he engaged in a more personalized attack against Betty: "You provoked this, always trying to get your way." The group session ended in chaos, with inappropriate name calling and an unnecessarily high degree of negative energy and commotion.

In the parenting group the leader helped Betty to review her negative experience with this event and thus to move beyond it. She used what had happened to point out to members the importance of communicating to one another with respect, whether leader or member. This meant listening intently to each other, and processing ideas carefully—in the group discussion among members, between a member and practitioner, between a member and her child(ren), and between a member and others in decision-making positions vis-à-vis children. Pondering the reasons for the practitioner's inappropriate behavior, the group wondered whether Betty's being female may have played a role: the constellation of male practitioner and female group may compound the power embodied in the leader role.[12] The group also considered the possibility that race played a part of the dynamic since some African-American males may feel under considerable pressure working with African-American women.[13] This unfortunate incident and the agency's response to it, which the practitioner reviewed with the group, illustrate the different levels of power and decision making that exist in this work.

Agency's Philosophy

The Mothers Moving Forward group and the Parenting Group for Recovering Addict Mothers were agency-based, programmatic efforts that implemented two rather different philosophical orientations. Mothers Moving Forward was developed in keeping with the agency's emphasis and focus on community and individual empowerment while the parenting group emphasized treatment and education.

As pivotal components of both agencies' programming, and consistent with their philosophy, these groups were held in attractive facilities and staffed by competent practitioners, one a highly capable MSW and the other a lay leader under the supervision of a master clinician who also had an MSW. The good fit between clients, setting, and group purposes that is key to insuring optimal growth and change was clearly in operation here. It is significant that both agencies held deep respect for these clients, as manifest in the fact that the practitioners consistently and in a caring way held the clients to high expectations for change within the groups and thus facilitated the movement of several members to higher functioning and better lives.

4

GROUP FORMATION AND DEVELOPMENT

Parenting Group for Recovering Addict Fathers

INTRODUCTION

In this presentation of a Parenting Group for Recovering Addict Fathers, we trace an intervention similar to that of the Parenting Group for Recovering Addict Mothers. The dynamics of the two groups differed not just because of the overwhelmed status of the men (it has been argued that their needs are often more pressing than those of overwhelmed women), but because of their attitudes toward the female practitioner and the subsequent power struggle with her. The men also proved to be more competitive in their relationships with one another than the women, who bonded more easily. Much of what we examined can be viewed as reactive behaviors based on faulty thinking, and responses to poverty and all the other facets of being overwhelmed. We also discuss the connection between culture and power and offer some empowerment intervention strategies. Another note: In all of our research on the overwhelmed featured here and in *The Power to Care* we found limited initiatives among the agencies focused on overwhelmed men and even fewer agencies that offered groups for this seriously disadvantaged population.

Group Compostion

The Parenting Group for Recovering Addict Fathers was organized in a manner similar to that of the corresponding mothers' group, which was discussed earlier. In other words, the format, recruitment and screening, and goals were nearly identical to the mothers' group and therefore are treated only briefly in this presentation. Both groups were formed and led by the same practitioner. The prospective members were all in recovery from alcohol or drug abuse.

Olivier: 33 years of age.

David: 38 years of age, married, father of five, HIV infected, and hoping to learn how to be a better husband and father. When he was abusing drugs he became largely unavailable to his wife and children.

Thomas: 28-year-old father of a nine-year-old son with whom he had no relationship; although he was frightened of the demands of his father role, he wanted to be a good father.

James: 29 years old, father of three, referred by DSS.

John Henry: 32-year-old father of six who could not read. All of his children were in state custody because his wife was in jail on drug charges.

George: At 48, the oldest member of the group. All of his children were in state custody. Employed as a taxi driver, unwilling to submit to urine test. Married.

G. Nelson: A 29-year-old father of a three-year-old daughter whom he adores. His girlfriend, the child's mother, represented an ongoing threat to the relationship he desired with his daughter. His alienation from the child's mother came as a result of a past history of both drug abuse and physical abuse.

Sol: 35 years of age, father of seven with whom he had minimal, if any, relationship owing to a drugging past and a 15-year period in and out of jail.

Ned: At 25, the father of a daughter 19 months old and a stepson three years old. Currently, the relationship with his companion is sometimes tumultuous.

Luis: A 42-year-old father of twins, a young girl and boy. Although not involved in a romantic relationship with the mother of the children, their relationship was such that he could visit with the twins.

Hugo: A 34-year-old married father of five whose wife and children offered support and encouragement. The oldest child, a 15-year-old girl, was the offspring of an earlier union whose mother made it difficult for him to assume the type of parental role that he desired with this daughter.

Recruitment and Screening

The eleven men listed above had been referred to the program by clinicians who were aware of the group and how others had benefited from the experience. Eight were African-American: David, Thomas, James, John Henry, G. Nelson, Sol, Ned and Hugo; Olivier was Haitian-American; Luis was Latino; and George was caucasian. All but George were currently involved in a drug treatment program.

Eight of the men attended the first session; Olivier and James had indicated to the practitioner that they would attend but did not. (The ninth, Hugo, joined at the fourth session after the group began.) In addition to maintaining sobriety, the goal of each member was to improve his parenting skills in order to be more successful in relationships with offspring. Relational issues loomed large for all the men, with their offspring, with their wives or companions, and with their families.

GROUP PROCESS

The Early Sessions: Goals, Contracts, and Agenda Building

As the men entered the agency they were each greeted warmly by the receptionist who directed them to the meeting room. There they were welcomed by the practitioner who offered coffee, tea, soda, cookies, and cake. As they stood around sipping drinks and snacking, she walked among them shaking hands and conveying how pleased she was to have them attend and how she wished for each a useful experience and an opportunity for growth. Shortly after the individual greetings they helped arrange their chairs in a circle. As soon as all were seated and quiet settled in the room, she began an opening ritual. Asking everyone to pause, she then intoned:

THINK. Think about the beauty of the day. Think about the opportunity we have. Think positive. Push out the negative thoughts, and the negative experiences of yesterday. Think positive about today and the weeks ahead.

There was a long pause after this introductory ritual which, based on principles of stress reduction, was designed to reduce personal and group tension and help members focus on the goals and task at hand.

Again she introduced herself and asked each member to identify himself. Some made brief comments about themselves after stating their names: "I was born right here in Boston," or "I just came to Boston a year or so ago, I grew up down south." Others were more reticent, giving only their names, then glancing downward.

The practitioner explained why the group was organized, emphasizing the goal of helping members learn about more effective parenting skills. Acknowledging their struggles with substance abuse, mostly cocaine, she underscored the importance of their maintaining sobriety, a prerequisite for initial as well as ongoing participation. A few of the members voiced their anxieties, sharing how they hoped the group could help. David, the AIDS-infected father of five, spoke out, asserting that while all present needed the group, they "needed Jesus in their lives more than anything." In this initial discussion he expressed his need to reconnect with his family, after being unavailable to his wife and children for the many years that he was heavily into cocaine. He declared that God was important in his life and shared his perspective that "All addicts could benefit from a close relationship to the Almighty."

John Henry, the father of six who had never learned to read, voiced enthusiasm for the group, and hoped that it could help him in his struggle to get his children back from the state. G. Nelson, an articulate member, expressed his fondness for his young daughter and the way in which he felt his goal was blocked by his former companion, the mother of his child with whom he no longer had romantic interest. Others nodded understanding and sympathy although they did not speak. Sol described his intent to attend all the sessions, asserting that "I am one hundred percent committed." Having been incarcerated for roughly 15 years, he acknowledged that he had little contact with his children.

With the introductions over, consensus reached regarding group purpose, individual goals clarified, and contracting completed, the practitioner asked if the members were ready to think about interactions within the group; how members would address one another and consider the importance of *respect* for one another during the sessions. In a very forthright manner she indicated that she expected them to be "gentlemen," meaning that each person must be carefully listened to and his contribution to the process responded to with care and respect. While the men voiced no disagreement at this time, the practitioner was well aware that there would be competition and conflict in the days ahead. She sensed some alienation in the very early moments of the first session when Dave became somewhat preachy.

In response to her questions they began to discuss their companions, children, other practitioners, and even the DSS workers, and she encouraged them to discuss these relationships in a respectful manner. This was consistent with their goal of becoming better parents despite such negative encounters as a fight with a girlfriend or a difficult, disappointing meeting with a DSS worker. The leader made it clear that discussions about these encounters were to be conducted without name calling. There would be no swearing. Speaking about their present or past companions and DSS staff (who were primarily women) without derogatory put-downs and profanity was a challenge for these men; nonetheless, the members nodded.

Informing them of the need to share responsibility for making their group process work, so that each could benefit, the practitioner stressed the importance of helping one another to reach personal as well as group goals. It was crucial, she emphasized, for the men to be open with one another and see the importance of sharing their experiences and responses. In addition to these manifest guidelines there were latent ones. For example, as noted earlier, it was agreed that members would address and relate to one another with respect. While there was no discussion about how members would refer to one another or to the practitioner, they began referring to one another by first names after introducing themselves in this way. Likewise, the practitioner referred to herself as Julia Brown and the men called her Ms. Brown.

Another tenet related to confidentiality. The practitioner counseled that all group talk must remain confidential. Whatever members shared was to remain in the confines of the room, not to be repeated at their homes, to friends, other practitioners, and even companions. Breach of confidentiality can be particularly problematic in a neighborhood setting. The sensitive nature of the members' problems was such that breaching this confidentiality could set them back in their attempts to reach their goals. If a group member heard something he had revealed about himself within the group repeated outside, the whole process would be compromised and possibly irreparably damaged. If, for example, a parent heard something unpleasant about himself in the form of gossip, his reaction could block opportunities for improving relationships with the children and/or companions. Moreover at times negotiations with the department of social services can be very sensitive, and it might not be in a family's best interest for an ugly exchange that had been discussed openly in a group session to get around the agency or the neighborhood.

Yet another tenet concerned the safety of members. The practitioner emphasized that all had an obligation to let her and appropriate staff know about any events that would endanger any member of the group, agency staff, or citizens. In this context it was necessary to make explicit that no weapons of any kind can be brought into the agency.

Other expectations dealt with the need for truthfulness and openness in discussion. Members were encouraged to think as honestly and accurately as possible about past events. The discouragement of manipulative, game-running behavior represented a new demand for many of these men. Their need to survive in a society in which they had been reduced to powerless roles—where they were perceived as largely useless except for fathering children—had pressed them to engage in a variety of power-over behaviors. Manipulation, domination, disrespect, and even violence had become ways to get a sense of power in the face of their perceived powerlessness. Many had experienced homelessness and had become street addicts having to finance uncontrollable appetites for drugs, mainly crack cocaine.

Once guides and norms were reviewed the practitioner handed out a printed statement that covered all items that had been taken up in discussion. Guidelines for the group were almost identical to those settled on for the Mother's Group (see Chapter 3).

The agenda suggested by the practitioner was one that had been used in previous parenting groups at the agency (also presented in Chapter 3.) She worked to encourage establishment of individual goals and group goals that were compatible, that would facilitate growth and reduce tension, including the potential for disruption. The men were eager to "get on with it," meaning they wanted immediately to focus on topics and instrumental tasks. Nonetheless the practitioner emphasized the importance of the group's process and the major goal, that of helping them become more competent in their role as fathers. An environment in which there was sharing of information, offering of support to one another, and the expectation of mutual aid was also a new experience for most of the men, given their life histories of isolation from their companions, wives, children, and parents.

One highly significant area of human functioning was missing for these men: work. Only one member, George, was employed, and as a cab driver. Thus, the connections and structure usually available to people in the workplace and the companionship with peer workers were nonexistent as supports. Though the men generally did not attend church and only one man spoke of connections to a church and spiritual community, some spoke of God's presence in their lives—a source for helping them stay the course in spite of challenges.

The Men: Their Struggles, Hopes and Goals

David expressed strong intent to get his life cleared up so that he could be a good husband and father. He regretted the time away from his family while he was drugging it up. He commented: "I came here to become a good father" and to "learn about parenting." Since God was in his life he was sure he would make it. Admitting to having marital difficulties and to some understanding as to why, given the difficulties stemming from his drugging past and the burdens that fell to his wife at that time, he stated that he and his wife were "trying to do better with" their relationship. Acknowledging that his first child was born when he was very young and that he had no understanding of the importance of limit set-

ting for children or how to set limits as a parent, he reflected that "drugs made matters worse." Though he often felt sad and overwhelmed about his struggle with AIDS, he could always pray and regain composure. It helped that whenever he spoke in the group about the suffering associated with AIDS, and about the medications and treatments, the men seemed to listen attentively and appeared to understand his pain and misery. His condition had also apparently helped him become more tuned in to others' pain and his empathy clearly showed as well as his wish that all should become religious.

John Henry was highly motivated and deeply concerned about his children since their mother had been put in jail because of drugs. Homeless, illiterate, and jobless, he talked about the hard road ahead. He asserted that he was determined to remain sober, learn to read and write, find housing, and get his children back from DSS. He also knew that he had to get a job. Though very positive and seemingly enthusiastic about change, John Henry was sometimes very quiet. He relied on the others for support, which they tried to offer, often by nodding or patting their feet. When the agency learned that he could not read or write, tutoring was made available. John Henry was pleased, studied hard, and later attempted to use his new skill during sessions. He would speak about the progress he was making in reading and how much better he felt now that he could read a little. His enthusiasm was contagious and his efforts were clearly applauded by the members. John Henry welcomed their support and encouragement; the bonding, camaraderie, and support became an important force in his life, and he never missed a session.

Sol acknowledged that he had a lot of work to do. What troubled him greatly was that he was the father of seven children but was alone and had no relationship with any of his offspring. Stating that he wanted to "find my kids," he reflected that drugs "destroyed my life," and that "doing fifteen years of time was a hard price." Now he wanted to get his life turned around, and asserted, "I am finished with crack. Don't want none of the stuff." When David commented that Sol needed prayer, the practitioner invited others to comment in an effort to steer discussion away from another sermon from David, who was always ready to tell the men that their faith was being tested. While the worker respected spiri-

tuality as a force in the group and allowed it to flourish, she was also committed to assuring that no one member monopolized the discussion and that no one would feel pressured in the group to do what someone else thought was right.

Ned was often an active contributor, though at times he too could be very quiet. He spoke lovingly about both his 19-month-old daughter and his three-year-old stepson who had recovered from serious burns suffered in a house fire, and it was obvious that he had a very warm spot for his infant daughter. As he described his struggles with her mother it became clear that the relationship was less than stable; however he felt that they both wanted "to do better because of the children." Ned would challenge opinions or suggestions offered to other members, often raising a question about them or suggesting alternative options. Although he was thoughtful, he was also aggressive, often pressing his point, and from time to time would become agitated, and even suggest that others should cease talking so much. He expressed this view about David, admonishing him to "stop preaching." What became increasingly obvious to the practitioner was that Ned really had a need to dominate discussion.

Thomas had a nine-year-old son with whom he had no contact, and although he clearly stated that nothing would please him more than reversing this situation, he was afraid to try. What frightened him was a fear that his attempt to develop a relationship with his boy might fail. Becoming readier to think about a positive relationship with his child and the joy that could be derived from fatherhood was something that Thomas shared with the other members.

G. Nelson talked about his daughter and how he wanted to have more time with her. He recognized that in order to be the kind of father he wanted to become would require that he learn how to get along with his former girlfriend. He spoke openly about the dilemma "of wanting to be with my daughter but not wanting to be with my old girlfriend." Commenting that "when I was high I might have hit my girlfriend and not treat her right but I don't do that no more," he claimed that she used his past behavior to get back at him. When their relationship was going well he was able to see his child but when they had disagreements his visits were blocked. He protested: "This is not fair." Once he had to petition the court in order to gain visitation rights, an action that proved very painful for him. Sensing his pain and sadness, David and John Henry offered verbal support, David again suggesting prayers.

George, the oldest in the group, became increasingly agitated as G. Nelson was speaking. With great emotion he spoke up, indicating that "outside control is terrible in a man's life," and commenting about how much he "hates the government's stepping into my life." He expressed disgust that G. Nelson had to go to court to get papers to see his own child. He went on to reveal how the government (the department of social services) was trying to force him to have regular urine tests and to attend the parenting group. George denied that he was an alcoholic, and he was convinced that DSS workers took his children without cause. He was also quite angry with his wife and blamed her, as well as the children, for his family's predicament. While it was initially difficult for George to open up, the support conveyed by the members and their understanding of his pain enabled George gradually to begin to offer support to the others, and to move into a more reciprocal style of relating. Nonetheless, the loss of control that members experienced in reference to their children and other aspects of their lives baffled George, who tended to handle his anger by intellectualizing the situation and scapegoating. Several of the men echoed George's resentments: the government was bad; their women made life miserable, betraying them, controlling the time they could spend with their children, and blocking them from being fathers.

The practitioner helped focus on the reality of their situation by asking such questions as "Why do you think your companions make things so difficult for you?" One or two of the men lashed out and others joined in, indicating that their women ought to be more understanding of a man's life and that even though they used drugs they should not have been denied visitation rights. Reluctant to acknowledge or accept responsibility for their drugging pasts and how drugs helped destroy their family life, several simply wanted to scapegoat others. George said that a man's woman should not turn on him when he was down and she should definitely not involve the government in family business. Again helping to focus on the social reality of their situations, the practitioner asked the men who would care for their children if they were able to share custody. John Henry commented that sometimes families might not make it without help, sharing again how his kids would have no place because both he and his children's mother used drugs which consumed most of their financial resources. There was little or nothing left for the children.

Hugo expressed how pleased he was to have some support from his wife and children, although managing relationships with the children posed a challenge. What was particularly problematic for him was his relationship with his oldest child, a 15-year-old daughter from a previous union. Noting that the girl's mother made it "very hard for me to see my *own* daughter," he asked the group for help and suggestions: "What do you all think I can do to get to see my daughter more?"

This was somewhat atypical because though Hugo usually had much to say about what the others should do, it appeared easier for him to offer advice than to receive it. Asking for help represented a behavior change. After a few men offered ideas, the practitioner complimented Hugo regarding his inquiry for assistance, and encouraged others to respond in a supportive manner. Hugo often tried to monopolize discussion, becoming competitive and boasting about his supportive wife and family, describing holidays the family spent together. This made him the recipient of some disapproval, and on occasion even a little hostility. Some of the feelings toward Hugo may have been a result of his late entry into the group, although the decision to permit him to join had been made by the men after what the practitioner considered to be thorough and careful deliberation. It seems more likely that the negative energy directed toward Hugo grew out of jealousy over his "advantage": his reported relationship with his wife which was more positive and stable than that experienced by others and also his "pretty boy" image, which he enjoyed exploiting. While Hugo was speaking several of the men reacted as if they doubted the description of his marriage and family life.

The practitioner reminded the men that each member should be allowed to discuss his issues and that all should listen carefully and not interrupt; there would be enough time for all to speak, and get "stuff" off of their chests. She found it necessary to make this comment more often here than in the mothers' parenting group. Mindful of the need to help keep the discussion focused but at the same time wanting to avoid gender-related power struggles, she was cautious but also direct. At times she moved the discussion ahead, ensuring that one member speak at a time and that all willing to speak would have the chance to do so. She did not allow the men to cut one another off, and often set limits, such as "Let G. Nelson finish, please," or "Thomas, did you finish your thought?"

On several occasions she noticed as she spoke that Ned would stare at her, and then hold his head down. Sensing some conflict or negative reaction toward herself and some feeling of both compassion and agitation toward other members, the practitioner struggled to identify what Ned was experiencing. There were times when other members appeared particularly silent; at such times getting them to open up required her to exert more initiative and energy. Sometimes she would ask the group to say why people might be quiet. Someone would reach for cake or fruit or milk and others would follow. Then people might become silly, laughing or teasing one another. Explanation about someone not participating fully in the program, an issue with staff, or a situation at home might surface. James offered that people were dealing with disappointments and were having a rough time.

> *Sol,* who had indicated in the first group session that he was "one hundred percent committed" and later told of his fifteen years away from his seven children while incarcerated, was an active participant when he came to the sessions. His insights about jail and his dangerous, fearsome street life served as vivid reminders that a life of drugs could be devastating. In all, Sol attended only four sessions. The practitioner later learned in her follow-up activities and feedback from the members that Sol had relapsed, and had been sent to a residential treatment facility.
>
> *Luis* entered the group after a brief period of sobriety, but unfortunately was not able to sustain freedom from drugs. After the second session word came that he had relapsed and he was unable to participate in the next six sessions. He successfully completed a detox program and

returned for the remaining four sessions, though he was never able to really connect with the members owing in large measure to the period of absence.

The Middle Phase

At midpoint (around the sixth session) there had now developed a pattern to the weekly process. The group might convene with the eight regular participants entering, helping themselves to snacks, then sitting in their usual positions waiting for the leader to start. On one occasion Ned beckoned: "Let's start." The men were shocked. No member had ever assumed this initiative. The strong nonverbal reaction of the men was such that Ned picked it up. The practitioner, however, was not so surprised, having noticed for several weeks his ongoing struggle for power and influence. She was also aware of the growing resistance to Ned, usually manifest through silent turnoffs and negative body language. G. Nelson spoke up, commenting that he expected Ms. Brown to open the session, and others, including David, John Henry, and George, agreed. Ms. Brown, in an effort to diffuse the tension and divert hostility from Ned, asked if the men wished to consider helping her prepare for the group and open the session. Even though they were competitive with one another and with the practitioner, it was clear from their responses that they were not yet ready for this instrumental type of leader role.

In a discussion on parenting skills that focused on gaining cooperation from children and managing anger, Hugo announced that he and his wife worked as a team. Since most others were alone, they listened with interest but soon grew tired of what they believed to be Hugo's boasting. G. Nelson asked Hugo what made him so successful in his relationship with his wife. He responded: "I treat her real fine, I just sent her flowers for Valentine's Day and took her out to dinner."

There was disbelief. Several men advised him to "Knock off the [expletives]," thinking that he was fabricating a story. G. Nelson spoke up again, saying how nice it must feel to be able to afford an expensive, romantic evening. What he was underscoring was the cost for an unemployed father. The men felt an explanation was required and Hugo could sense the doubt of the members. Their reactions may also have expressed jealousy. Ned pointedly asked, "Where did you go for dinner?" And David, trying to bring a positive tone to the discussion, commented that he wished he could do the same and that with the Almighty's help, he hoped he would live to take his wife out next year.

Redirecting the discussion, the practitioner suggested that members might discuss a different issue, namely, how to gain cooperation from their children and spouses. G. Nelson stated that he did fine with his child, but that his problem was managing the relationship with his ex, who he was convinced blocked him from visitation because of spite and anger over his decision to call off their relationship. He asked the group, "How am I going to deal with her?"

David suggested praying, which annoyed Ned and George, who were interested in more immediate and concrete approaches. G. Nelson made it clear that he wanted to know what steps to take. He didn't want to go back to court. The practitioner, who had always taken the position that all approaches would be nonviolent, responded that now perhaps it would be useful for the group to discuss negotiation strategies that might be useful to everyone. From time to time she had reminded the group of the importance of nonviolent behavior, but there had been no discussion of examples.

She asked G. Nelson to think about different ways to approach his former companion. Others were asked to think hard also. G. Nelson suggested: "I could ask her to talk with me. I could say that I won't get mad—talk bad and stuff."

Thomas asked about how to stay cool. George reflected that it was sad that G. Nelson had to beg to see his child. John Henry said that a man should be able to see his child—regardless.

Deciding to try a role play, the practitioner asked G. Nelson to speak as if he was communicating to his child's mother. He complied:

I'd like to talk with you about my child. I want to see her. I need to talk to you.

The practitioner asked the men how many ever thanked the women for caring for their children. This provoked the thought that such a thank-you might be included in an initial call for arranging visitation.

Similarly, the practitioner helped the men frame requests free of criticism and attack. For example, they were alerted to the potential of set-backs if they started out saying such things as:

You keep me from my child. You always have your way—never let me see my child. You no good—trying to keep me from my children.

This role playing continued as other men tried their skill at negotiation with an old girlfriend, a child, and eventually a DSS worker.

These role-playing exercises helped the men learn how to focus on constructive ways to behave and to achieve their goals: not swearing, staying cool, and not attacking. The men were learning how not to use abuse, violence, and other power-over behaviors that had been their automatic response to feeling pain, being overwhelmed, and being forced into powerless roles.

As the group progressed, it became increasingly clear how possessive the men were of their children, no matter how tenuous the connection. A child or children represented their only major accomplishment and became a significant driving force behind the conflict and competition, fighting, struggle, and abuse between them and their children's mothers. Moreover, it soon became clear to the practitioner that for some of the men, the continued conflict with a child's mother became a source of connection, attention, and a way of feeling involved with the child—albeit a negative source.

Turning this negative thinking and this conflict-laden behavior around became a primary goal in the work of the group. To achieve these goals the practitioner had to demonstrate how to change their usual responses to powerlessness into competent self-affirming, conflict-resolving behaviors. Thus, role playing and talking out positive responses that encourage conflict-free dialogue and behavior become an important part of this relearning. This requires time, effort, and repetition. The practitioner must listen attentively while coaching the members, who must learn to develop better listening skills as they learn new strategies for dialogue—that is, to speak and not attack. In this context the men were learning how to take risks and even to tolerate being vulnerable as a source of strength and competence instead of viewing these stances as indications of "cowardice."

A note: On more than one occasion the practitioner did identify ways in which women blocked opportunities for the men to see their children, often unnecessarily provoking them. Unfortunately these mothers were not involved in any helping relationship, either group or individual, that might encourage them to change these behaviors.

Ending Phase

As the group evolved and learned new approaches for conflict resolution and conflict avoidance some of the earlier dynamics ceased. For example, when Ned attempted to take over the group he had been demonstrating a need to be in control and take power from the female leader. Allowing a woman to have a positive leadership role without put-downs, fighting, and abuse had been a new demand. Accepting such a role represented a new level of growth and was manifested by the end of the group experience.

Another member attempted to exert control over the leader through seduction. Earlier in the group process the practitioner had pondered the meaning of this member's intense stares, which were accompanied by stillness in body posture and an absolute lack of motion. What she discovered through discussion with him individually was that he perceived himself "to have a crush" on her. She saw this effort to seduce her as a way of trying to gain mastery and control. She was able to see to it that he understood that such a power-over relationship with the leader was off limits but that he learned through this experience that he could participate and grow within the boundaries of a professionally led group.

Most of the men made progress in their efforts to become better parents. They demonstrated improved communication skills and were invested in improving relationships with their children and companions. These were enhanced by their new comprehension of the importance of avoiding power-over behaviors, and the value of negotiation.

Most importantly, there was only one member who relapsed and remained in the drugging life style; yet another member fell back but with professional intervention was able to return and complete the remaining group sessions. Bravo for sobriety! Although the fathers in this group never bonded as did the women in the mothers' parenting group, they did develop camaraderie and a level of support, very new experiences for most.

Assisting group members to move from the supportive relationships in the group into new collateral ones in the environment was an important task for the leader. In both women's groups (Women Moving Forward and the Parenting Group for Recovering Addict Mothers) this was also the case. However, the women also had prospects for jobs, community college, and volunteer service. For these fathers, life was clearly different: there were no solid prospects for employment, job training, or even education at the time the session ended. The practitioner, extremely concerned about this state of affairs, lamented:

> What are they going to do? Without some training and the hope of a job it might be back to drugs. They need to be able to at least hope for a brighter future.

She went on to comment that the men were realistic and knew that they had much personal work to accomplish before they could get a job, but that their despair at the lack of opportunity for jobs and training held them back.

DIRECTIVE LEADER SKILLS

The practitioner was not only skilled in group dynamics but worked effectively in a group with men that most of society generally viewed as useless. She demonstrated capability in handling verbal conflict and intense power struggles characterized by emotional and psychological depletion. She was able to engage the men in the group, keep them coming, and help them attain self-respect and new ways of behaving that facilitated their relational skills, especially with their partners and children.

We have postulated that in work with groups of overwhelmed clients the practitioner will often need to assume an assertive, directive-leader role. As shown from the groups described thus far, this is in contrast to the traditional nondirective role usually adopted by the practitioner. Several forces make it necessary for the practitioner to assume a more directive stance with this population. First, the needs of clients are often critical and immediate, mobilizing a different sense of urgency for the practitioner. As noted earlier, the need to help an unemployed homeless man, or a drugging father, dictates a certain response to reality that suggests immediacy.

Second, overwhelmed clients come from families beset by so many traumatic conditions that they have too often become either leaderless and underorganized[1] or led by persons who overfunction and become dominating and overly controlling in order to compensate for the chaos around.[2]

Third, the psychological condition of clients depleted of emotional resources due to the need to feed a drug appetite, for example, can be such that they lack the necessary confidence in their capacity to participate in a group and therefore need more than the usual supports to begin the process. An AIDS-infected former addict with a wife and five children has faced such tough reality that his sense of hope, let alone self-confidence, barely exists. It becomes the task of the practitioner to help rebuild such shattered lives within the group process.

In addition to psychological devastation this population also suffers from financial impoverishment. Note that several had lost custody of their children to the state, a situation often associated with hopelessness, powerlessness, and depletion of financial resources. In many instances where children were not in custody of the state and were placed in a foster care, they were in the home of a relative who received support for the children from the state. In such instances relatives who form an attachment often find it hard to release the children, creating other stressors.

In groups where clients are not overwhelmed with such realities practitioners can often be nondirective, creating an atmosphere where individuals can feel free to express themselves openly. In such situations the nonjudgmental, open, democratic, accepting, empathic postures of the practitioner are helpful attributes for moving these groups ahead.[3]

With the overwhelmed, the task becomes more complex: these same leader attributes are necessary but also needed is the capacity to take a more directive role because of the conditions noted already. As discussed earlier a major goal in the Women Moving Forward group and in both the mothers' and fathers' parenting groups was to help members move to democratic, problem-solving functioning within the group.

TABLE 4–1

Directive Leadership in Groups for the Overwhelmed

- Aggressive outreach through schools, recreation programs (e.g., mothers and children on playgrounds), substance abuse programs, churches, etc.)
- Careful assessment and enrollment
- Follow-up (needed for population where systems have failed, clients have been made to feel unwelcome, population has no reason to trust systems)
  —Calling to remind members of meeting
- Careful pre-meeting planning
  —Multicultural practices (e.g., bilingual posters)
  —Arranging for warm hospitable greetings by receptionist
  —Offering coffee, tea, cakes, sandwiches, and yogurt (recognizing potential for hunger)
- Explicit statement of group purpose
- Explicit statement of guidelines (used as a handout)
- Careful monitoring
- Clear, explicit goal setting and contracting
  — Swearing is off limits
  — Aggressive behavior is off limits
- Clear commitment obtained from members to abide by contract
  —I will not swear
  —I will not fight
- Direct intervention in process
  —Explaining democratic values
  —Keeping discussion focused and allowing all members opportunity to speak
  —Setting limits; emphasis on *respect* and appropriate behaviors
  —Managing/redirecting conflict and power battles
  —Discouraging power-over behaviors
  —Teaching and role-playing negotiating skills
  —Respect for others' needs, listening and using positive appropriate language
  —Commitment to safety for self and all group members (essential for functioning of the group)

GENDER DIFFERENCE

In Chapter 3 we called attention to some differences between the two parenting groups. In the father's group, the following differences were noted, indicating a more directive practitioner approach:

- Greater need for emphasis on respect
- Direct limitations on swearing, name calling, and general put-down behavior
- Greater emphasis on explaining need for confidentiality
- Direct prohibition against weapons
- Direct prohibition against violence and abusive behavior
- Greater emphasis on need for truthfulness and openness
- Greater emphasis on need to help one another

The practitioner expended more energy in the effort to help the fathers do what came more easily to the mothers—that is, being helpful to one another and opening up. The mothers were not as verbally or physically aggressive and they related to the practitioner initially in a manner that suggested they had greater readiness for group interaction.

OUTCOME

Notwithstanding these gender differences, the fathers' group members showed progress in the growth of skills necessary for higher social functioning. Of note is the fact that a larger number of fathers attended regularly—eight out of eleven; while five out of twelve mothers attended regularly—though the fathers never bonded as tightly as mothers. Also the fact that both groups were part of an array of services offered by the agency contributed to the attendance, participation, and cohesion. It may have been far more challenging to start a group that was not part of an existing program.

CULTURE AND POWER

It is important in work with all overwhelmed clients for practitioners to understand the connection between culture and power, and it is crucial in work with overwhelmed men, who as noted earlier seem even more isolated in this society than overwhelmed women.

Overwhelmed clients frequently seek assistance from practitioners whose culture differs from theirs. Key to effectiveness in this work is practitioners' competence to work with such clients. Competence re-

TABLE 4–2

Empowerment Intervention Strategies

- Contextualize the problem—Understand how the social system has impacted one's behavior
- Identify behavioral responses to powerless roles
- Understand survival nature of such behaviors; identify strengths
- Understand reactive nature of these responses to powerless roles: Understand costs
    (Can't set own goals, plan, take leadership except in reactive ways)
- Connect faulty thinking to antisocial behavior
- Set personal (and group) goals
- Take responsibility for reactive behavior that blocks teaching goals
- Learn proactive, prosocial behaviors
  —Change faulty thinking
  —Change antisocial behaviors
- Learn to exercise power effectively: Be a leader
- Learn to function in collaborative roles, negotiate
- Learn to take action in community as a citizen, advocate, voter, change agent

quires respect for and knowledge of the clients' culture, and the capacity to help them, as group members, to respect one another's culture. This opportunity to learn and demonstrate mutual respect while in the group can and hopefully will be carried over into other experiences.

Practitioners' knowledge of their own culture should include the capacity to take responsibility for managing any biases, prejudices, learned misinformation, and distorted attitudes and stereotypes held about clients. Each client must be given the opportunity to demonstrate his or her own strengths. The flexibility in thinking and behavior that such a stance requires means that extra steps, extra effort, and extra time will be needed to understand the differences presented by the client. This means using a way of thinking that involves application of general knowledge about various cultural groups to a specific client. A two-level process which involves a look at the specifics within the general and vice versa, while managing the complexities involved, is a key to empowering.[4] In the next chapter, we will illustrate how differences within a specific ethnic group can pose a challenge for practitioners who are called upon to understand varying and conflicting perceptions of a given group. For example, in the University Women of African

Descent group, after some conflict between black Hispanic and African-American women in the group, the practitioners were required to help members process the meaning of friendship in Latino and African-American culture and to help them understand that despite their differing perceptions of one another's groups, the larger community viewed them as the same: black!

Understanding in all of its ramifications also includes reaching a comfort level vis-à-vis gender differences and differences in sexual orientation (heterosexual, homosexual, and bisexual). An open attitude is required for skillful, new-age practitioners.

Table 4.2 on empowerment intervention strategies identifies several approaches. Most have been used in groups thus far and will be seen in the following vignettes as well.

5

WOMEN'S AND CHILDREN'S GROUPS

Vignettes

INTRODUCTION

In this chapter we use social group vignettes to focus on different aspects of group practice with a variety of populations: (1) older Vietnamese women; (2) women of African descent on the campus of a major American university; and (3) well children whose parent or parents are suffering with HIV/AIDS. The groups are unique in a number of ways. The literature does not often focus on Vietnamese groups because it is generally assumed that cultural constraints keep them from easily joining with others, opening up, and participating in a support group. The University Women of African Descent group shows how group process can facilitate coping with developmental issues which are influenced by cultural dynamics and a new environment. Finally, the group for well children who live with parents or other family members suffering from HIV/AIDS demonstrates work with a population that is largely forgotten.

Particular attention is given to the role of the professional facilitator in each of these groups. Readers will note that although discussion about the groups covers similar topics, there is some variation since two were ongoing and one was time limited and also because practitioners focused on different issues and themes.

WOMEN SAVING FACE

Purpose and Formation

The purpose of this long-term group was to provide support to eight Vietnamese women transitioning from one culture to another.[1] This group was unique in that it required a translator who functioned as a pivotal member of the intervention team. The group was co-led by two practitioners, one of whom was a supervisor.

Recruitment and Screening

Each member of the group had experienced problems in adjusting to American culture and had been evaluated for and determined to be suffering from depression and/or PTSD (post-traumatic stress disorder). All participants had felt a sense of alienation and powerlessness consequent to their traumatic experiences in Vietnam and to stress relating to immigration. An increasing number of Vietnamese Americans experience such alienation, a problem that is ranked third among the six top problems they face. The only two problem areas that loom larger than alienation are the loss of role identity and self-esteem.[2] Members of the group were referred from an agency-sponsored Vietnamese social group that met on a weekly basis in a senior center. Since they were all familiar with this agency, which supplies culturally sensitive services for Vietnamese-Americans, members knew the purpose of the group prior to referral.

In referring members to the group, the practitioners were mindful of the commonalities shared by each: age range, gender, ethnic origin, and similarities in life experience related to war, trauma, and refugee-immigration status. Loss of family and village and struggle with pain and guilt over having left their children in the old homeland were experiences these women had in common.[3]

The group members were also viewed by their neighbors as part of a new wave of immigrants of color moving into formerly all-white ethnic residential areas. The projection of minority status on these women (i.e., as immigrants of color) was a new experience, since in their homeland, although they had been victims of communism and the destructiveness of war, they had not been required to deal with status based on race.

They also struggled with concepts of care and definitions of mental health that differed drastically from those they had known in Vietnam.[4]

Contracting for Goals

The group sought to empower these members, older Vietnamese immigrant women, through facilitating personal growth and enhancing their capacity to (1) adapt to their new environment, including mastering of English; (2) grow stronger through common sharing of past traumatization and current acculturation issues; (3) cope with loss and isolation owing to having left children and other family back in their homeland; and (4) manage intense and immobilizing anger in relation to (a) political changes in the old country that had led to the destruction of family and community and (b) changes in the behavior of husband and children who were now operating under a different set of role expectations in their new country.

Group Composition

The eight members of the group ranged in age from 59 to 74.

> *Ms. O. was a 61-year-old Vietnamese woman living in the United States for political reasons since 1993. She came with her husband who had been imprisoned in Vietnam for 14 years before immigrating to this country. His lengthy prison term, which had warranted priority for immigration, left Ms. O. to care and protect six young children, the oldest of whom had been forced to serve in the Cambodian Army. Two of Ms. O.'s children now reside in the United States, while four are still in Vietnam. Trying to adjust to her new culture by learning English has been difficult as she has memory problems and can't remember what she has been taught in Western culture.*
> *Ms. E. was a 66-year-old Vietnamese woman who came to the United*

States in 1995, six years after her husband. She raised four children who are in their early 40s now and still live in Vietnam. She recently secured her daughter's immigration to the United States and her daughter will be moving here with her family in about one year. Ms. E. and her husband are raising their 16-year-old grandson. This has been a source of stress for both of them as they perceive a lack of respect from their "American" grandson, behavior very different from how he might have been as a teenager in Vietnam. A shift in social status after the Communist takeover of Vietnam had also left both Ms. E. and her husband, who had been better respected in their homeland, experiencing additional stress in relation to the demands of adjusting to U.S. societal ways.

Ms. U. was a 74-year-old Vietnamese woman who came to the United States in 1995. She and her husband escaped from Vietnam by boat to a refugee camp in Malaysia. Ms. U. had few freedoms in the camp and was jailed briefly for stealing food. All seven of Ms. U.'s children now live in the United States, having moved here a few years before she and her husband arrived. Ms. U.'s main reason for leaving Vietnam was to be with her children. Since living here, though, she had been disappointed by their lack of attention and respect toward her and her husband. Her expectations of them were continually shattered, as they do not provide financial help or other instrumental assistance.

Ms. B. was a 59-year-old Vietnamese woman who had lived in the United States with her two children since 1992. Both of Ms. B.'s parents died when she was young, leaving Ms. B. on her own by the age of 12. Her first husband had left her because she never became pregnant. Her second marriage, to an older Chinese man with whom she had two children, ended after a few years when her husband died while he was in another country visiting another woman. Because her children had not been "full Vietnamese," she was treated with little respect in her community. Ms. B. has expressed frustration about the lack of professional counseling support services for citizens of Vietnam.

Ms. V. was a 65-year-old Vietnamese woman who came to the United States in 1995. Her husband had been an officer in Vietnam and was imprisoned from 1975 until his death in 1982. Ms. V. had five children, all of whom were in the United States. She lived with three of them. Ms. V. harbored intense anger and resentment toward the politi-

cal regime in Vietnam which had barred her and her children from legal employment. To survive during the war, she sold vegetables while her children fixed bicycles.

Ms. I. was a 68-year-old Vietnamese woman who came to the United States in 1995 with her husband and five of her ten children. Unlike the other members of the group, she was from a farming community, and the other five children remained to continue cultivating the farm. Being separated from these children had been devastating for her. It had taken months before she could talk about them without breaking down and sobbing. She had begun to write to them on a regular basis and was now able to find some comfort in talking to them on the telephone.

Ms. A. was a 66-year-old Vietnamese woman who came to the United States in 1993 with her four children. After being in the group for a year, Ms. A. revealed that she had never been married to her children's father (who had died in 1975) and that she had harbored much shame around this. Ms. A. was beginning to understand English fairly well and had been taking English classes at a local community college. She took much pride in this and in her daughter's current enrollment in college.

Ms. G. was a 61-year-old Vietnamese woman who came to the United States in 1992. In Vietnam her husband had been imprisoned and had suffered brain damage from torture. She thus had to raise her three young children alone and supported her family by selling drinks on the street along with her brother. When her husband was finally released from jail, she and her family escaped to avoid being sent to a labor camp. After coming to the United States, her children had less time for her. This was a particularly distressing state of affairs because of what she calls her husband's "mental illness" and also because she was unable to negotiate the system for his care because of language and cultural barriers.

GROUP PROCESS

Early Phase

Because these older Vietnamese women were coping with a new environment and dealing with past trauma and loss, practitioners helped each member to connect their personal problems with larger issues in the United States and on the international scene. The process, contextualization of members' problems, began with a review of the group's goals: to overcome language barriers and to learn to deal with cultural nuances, both of which could slow the process of change. Practitioners used a relational model of group dynamics which emphasizes empowerment, overcoming powerlessness, and members' connection to one another as manifested by putting themselves in the other's place—known as mutual empathy.[5] In this model there is emphasis on the value of hearing and accepting the client's definition of the problem, building on a client's strength and resources, conducting a power analysis of the client's situation which focuses on having each member identify the current and daily concerns and problems in order to understand how these events have helped shape her present sense of powerlessness.

Middle Phase

The assumption that Asian women are reluctant to open up, coming from cultures that emphasize privacy and self-control,[6] and thus are poor candidates for group membership, actually was the case initially. However once a safety zone was created the women in this group became eager to share their experiences. One member, Ms. A., after extensive encouragement by the leader, tearfully shared the deeply painful secret she had kept to herself most of her life. When she was young, long before she left her village, she had become involved with an older man, bearing a child. They had formed a family and, despite their lack of legal or religious sanction, had three other children. This "secret" had been overwhelming in its impact upon her self-value, forcing her into physical and emotional isolation as she attempted to avoid the shame associated with unmarried motherhood. Decades later, now in a distant country, away from family, old friends, and village elders, and as a member of a group of women so like those whom she had avoided back home, Ms. A. had a chance to free herself from this shameful burden. The practitioners, recognizing that "allowing members to become more intimate within the group by revealing their pain can encourage group development,"[7] helped the members to support Ms. A., permitting time for them to show comfort and consolation. Her risk taking and "the placing of her secret in perspective"[8] made it less difficult for others to begin thinking about unloading their troublesome issues. The group became so affirming and cohesive that it became difficult to schedule vacations and other times when the group would not meet because of the members' eagerness to keep it going.

Moreover, these women came from a culture that had extended fewer rights to females than exist in the United States. However, although women here in the States have less limited roles than those in Vietnam, both groups experience barriers and roadblocks.[9]

Given the degree of pain experienced by the women in this group and the depression and sense of powerlessness they had experienced as immigrants in a new country, it was remarkable that they had not been immobilized. But despite their burden of loss, pain, and trauma, and although they were now senior in age, they retained the capacity to come into the agency, make adjustments to the new culture, and even begin to learn a new language.

Part of their adjustment required adaptation to this country's youth-dominated, future-oriented society, one with very different values and cultural practices from theirs, in which the elderly had been held in deep respect, even reverence.[10] Loss of opportunity to enjoy the status inherent to the role of elder citizen in their culture was for them a serious disappointment and created a sense of personal loss.

Outcome

Monitoring process and documenting outcome are expectations in today's managed health care environment. With these groups, the co-practitioners did attempt to assess effectiveness of their process through the use of two evaluation instruments: the Hopkins Symptom Checklist and the Geriatric Depression Scale.[11] These instruments were administered in Vietnamese by the group's translator to the individual members. Depression was not found despite manifestations of such in group members, which means that more relevant quantitative instruments are needed.[12]

Using a Translator in Group Process

Translator-assisted groups facilitate the acculturation process and provide the immigrant with an opportunity to learn participation in a new society. In the future, the need for translators is expected to increase because of the escalating numbers of political refugees and new immigrants.[13] Since the presence of a translator does change the dynamics of the group process, group leaders must become comfortable in working with the different process that results when another such team member is added.

The high potential for misunderstanding and conflict among group members as they attempt to communicate with one another and with the leader creates a sense of caution in this population. The multilevel aspect of verbal and nonverbal communication carries a vulnerability for miscommunication to occur in the group process whenever more than one person feels compelled to communicate at any one time. The possibility of miscommunication in such situations is even further compounded by the process of translation. Since group members did not speak English and group leaders did not speak Vietnamese, their communication with one another had to take place via translator. Under such circumstances it was important that all members have a chance to express their concerns about a process that seemed foreign to them. Being able to discuss what it meant to speak in their own language—one different from that of the leader—to respond to the leader's invitation to members to express their honest reactions, enhanced their confidence and trust in the leader. Such a strategy can serve as a model for listening and accepting the feedback of other members.

The pace of communication is slowed considerably when translation is necessary. Because translation is a two-way process—from members to practitioners and back—communication takes at least twice as long as in non-translator-assisted groups. Moreover, practitioners must rely more heavily on nonverbal aspects of communication to help them understand what the client is trying to convey. Tone of voice, manner of speaking, speed of speech, and so on must be closely attended to in order to comprehend what members are experiencing and expressing. For example, according to the practitioner whose work we investigated, when members are discussing painful events such as loss of family, the discomfort they experience can cause them to respond in a rapid, fast-paced manner such that the translator can miss significant parts of the content. Of course, this may be the intent of the communicator. To cope with this impediment to the process, the practitioner, noticing the body language, would draw attention to the members' behavior, commenting on it in a way that conveyed her understanding of their discomfort and sense of isolation, which she would suggest mirrored her own. Gradually they began to talk about what it meant to be excluded because of language barriers and other cultural differences. By sharing her own sense of isolation and her own vulnerability in relation to the language and cultural barriers, the practitioner facilitated for these women a sense of being empowered, which was an experience that had been missing in their lives. In remaining culturally aware, and in remaining attentive to the Vietnamese cultural proscription against opening up, and to nuances, inflection in speech, and body language, the practitioner thus manifested respect for the members. This even involved moving into a one-down position at times, and staying away from direct confrontation.

Translators enjoy a unique power position in relation to both the practitioner and the group members. In this case the translator, in committing herself to the goals of both the group members and the practitioners, stood ready to facilitate members' growth and did not compete with or usurp the practitioner role.

Not to be minimized is the trust factor between the practitioner and the translator. The translator has the responsibility of ensuring that translations be carefully done in relation to time and feeling, using neither exaggeration nor understatement: a serious responsibility.

Several styles of interpreting have been identified, including verbatim translation at one end of the continuum, where the interpreter assumes the role of a conduit between the practitioner and the client, to that of independent interviewer, where the interpreter might dominate the process, at the other end. Resting somewhere in between these poles is the team approach, where the interpreter is viewed as part of the intervention team.[14] In the example above, the interpreter was a respected team participant whose knowledge of Vietnamese language and culture was coupled with an understanding of the purpose and goals of the group that made her contribution very valuable. The interpreter helped the practitioners through complexities associated with both verbal and nonverbal communication: knowing the meaning of

certain body movements, rapid, fast-paced chatter or quiet, low-key reactions—behaviors that were all demonstrated from time to time. The
translator's function was not unlike the role of cultural consultant described by Freed in her explanation of cross-cultural interviewing and
the use of an interpreter:

> The function is appropriately interpreting the communications and also
> helping to bridge cultural value difference between patient and therapist.
> At times they set aside the role of interpreter to evaluate the content of
> what is being translated and thus fulfill a cultural consultant role.[15]

Role of Supervisor

Another dimension in this equation was the supervisor. A member of
the dominant culture, she herself had been educated at a doctoral level
and was well prepared to appreciate the many complexities involved in
conducting a successful process with a group such as this. Culture, language, class, age range of members, and the dynamics involved in transition from Vietnamese village to large American city, along with the
pain internalized as a result of war, trauma, and loss, were among the
issues with which the group was struggling. This supervisor had prior
experience working with other clients who had left children and family
behind in their native countries, thereby losing the role of mother, a
major source of self-esteem.

USING LITERATURE TO EMPOWER UNIVERSITY WOMEN
OF AFRICAN DESCENT

Purpose and Formation

The purpose of this group was to provide an appropriately safe, supportive environment that would help students of African descent who
were struggling with issues and problems related to self-development,
personal relationships, and adjustment to life at a predominately white
university. The group was structured to use

> certain activities which are especially useful in bringing to the surface pow-
> erful emotions that are experienced but not articulated by group members.

Because the focus of such activities is on the activity itself, and not the person, participants are more willing to share their feelings during these activities.[16]

Literature was used in this group as such a tool to encourage discussion and mobilize group process and interaction that could facilitate a sense of support and growth for members. The group leaders preselected the works to be examined, all of which were written by highly acclaimed African-American women. Addressing themes relevant to the experience of this population, the literature includes such works as *Sisters of the Yam* by bell hooks,[17] *Mama* by Terry McMillan,[18] and *The Wedding* by Dorothy West.[19] Authors were also selected because they could serve as successful role models, having overcome handicaps and roadblocks in writing and publishing.

Recruitment and Screening

This group, which was voluntary and time-limited, met each semester in ten scheduled ninety-minute sessions conducted during the academic calendar year, September through May. Members were recruited through a university-sponsored newsletter, the university's counseling service, and by word of mouth. The newsletter carries information on group purpose (i.e., a support group for women of African descent), eligibility criteria, time and location of sessions, and name of the contact person. Applicants were assessed in terms of readiness to participate in the group via an intake form and an intensive interview conducted jointly by the two group leaders. Topics covered in the one-hour interview included previous group experience, previous experience with mental health counseling or treatment, and motivation for participation in the group.

More than half of the applicants were rejected for reasons such as severe depression, inability or unwillingness to make a ten-week commitment to the group, and serious relational issues as manifest in conflict and competition with other women and/or companions. When information indicated the presence of serious relational problems or when behavior was observed to be marked by deficiencies in social skills, or tendencies to engage in aggressive behavior toward others, alternative supports were suggested and in some instances referral was made to the university counseling service with an agreement for reevaluation after sufficient individual work had been completed. In other words, the old saw, ". . . starting where the client is" was an important consideration.[20]

For example, two coeds, both students of color but one black Hispanic and one African-American, had become embroiled in conflict that had ended in a serious public dispute. During the screening interview of one of these students, it was immediately apparent to the leaders that the young woman, who ostensibly had come to the group for help, intended the group to provide a bully pulpit for rallying support against the other. At the time, many students had been aware of the conflict and were taking sides, creating tension in the dorm and other congregate facilities.

The group leaders referred this candidate to university support services, suggesting that conflict mediation might be a more appropriate service, and encouraged her to reapply after she had worked through this crisis. She did so and became a member of a later group. Given the sensitive nature of issues gripping the campus and the need for the group endeavor to be viewed as open, the leaders worked to prevent the group from becoming entangled in an open, widely polarized debate.

The women selected were those who manifested interest in self-development, were motivated to work at improving relationships with peers, family, and companions, and showed capacity for self-disclosure and growth. The group leaders were a Ph.D. psychologist, Kathy Williams, and a Ph.D. candidate in social work, Betsy Taylor.

Contracting for Goals

The goals of the group centered on empowering women of African descent on a white-majority university campus to function more adequately in a competitive environment by facilitating improvement in self-awareness, self-esteem, social skills, and relational skills. Accomplishment of these goals required attention to the context in which these students found themselves as well as to their own behavioral responses. All entered in a contract to achieve these goals.

Group Composition

Ellie is a 20-year-old junior and an education major who is Haitian.

Shasta is an 18-year-old freshman and an education major who is Jamaican.

Tanasha is a 21-year-old senior and a sociology major who is African-American.

Katrina is a 21-year-old and a psychology major who is biracial and who identifies herself as African-American.

Kahi is a 21-year-old senior and a political science and black studies major who is African-American.

Tiffany is a 20-year-old sophomore and a management major who is African-American.

Kathy is a 20-year-old sophomore and an education major who is biracial and who identifies herself as African-American.

All of the group members were students receiving some type of financial aid, which they were supplementing by part-time work, with the exception of one, Kathy, who was receiving assistance from her family. All except Kathy, who resided in a West Coast suburb, were from poor or working-class urban families living on the East Coast.

GROUP PROCESS

Early Phase

The first meeting was viewed as the "icebreaker" where members and leaders were introduced. An art activity called "four corners" was utilized to help members feel comfortable and begin the "opening up" process. Participants were asked to make comments on preselected topics through writing and drawing.

The four topics about which group members shared ideas, beliefs, and experiences in writing and in drawing centered on family, women, campus life, and personal issues. The drawing exercise helped them to relax and think about themselves within a context that was both supportive and challenging. Issues that surfaced in relation to these women included concerns with teenage pregnancy and how it affects the future life chances of a young person, workplace relationships, male/female relationships, and how to find "Mr. Right."

Campus life issues included topics related to competition and conflict with peers, some of which had been fueled by racial differences. Group members had felt intense discomfort and a sense of racial isolation related to the lower status accorded them in comparison to their white counterparts. Participants were seeking assistance with how to handle the ongoing put-downs driven by race and social class differences that they frequently experienced.

Family issues included unresolved conflicts with parents and siblings, and expectations regarding financial support while in college. It is not unusual for students who use family funds for education to feel guilty if other family needs are going unmet, for siblings to feel competitive toward the one receiving family largesse, or for the family to feel burdened. Other concerns included issues about post-college life—for example, whether or not to return to inner-city life after exposure to life on a comparatively safe university campus. Sometimes these issues were highly emotionally charged. In one instance a member had difficulty discussing her family. Betsy suggested that she draw a picture. When her drawing of her family included only her mother and she was questioned about her father she commented: "He was a sperm-donor, not a father."

After the issues had been identified and discussed, the group members were asked to consider what personal goals and self-development objectives they would like to set for themselves. Betsy introduced this task thusly:

> I want you to think hard about how *you* can grow and what *you* can achieve personally in ten weeks. Write yourself a letter addressing personal goals and expectations that you think should be derived from this experience. You may wish to start the letter after this initial session and work on it through the coming weeks. The content of the letter is shared voluntarily and only at the last session.

A list of typical personal goals and expectations that were identified show a range of interest:

- To develop greater self-esteem and personal confidence

- To develop sound and positive relationships with persons of African descent and others of differing ethnic and racial background
- To identify and strengthen personal competencies

While there were goals for the group, there were also those for each individual member.[21] These personal goals also tended to be widely shared.

During the first session, Betsy asked whether members were ready to examine one of the specific concerns identified during the four corners exercise. Tanasha spoke first about the issue of campus relationships:

I am concerned about the way we treat one another: on this campus, in our communities, and in general. The put-downs, scorn, and hate are bad.

Other members echoed Tanasha's sentiments. Sensing from their empathic responses that Tanasha had identified a critical area of concern, the leaders encouraged other comments.

Kathy said, "There is no sense of unity on this campus; everybody is doing something totally different to reach the same goal."

Ellie commented, "I think some of us believe that they are better than others. I mean, I go out of my way to converse or just say 'Hi!' to other black sisters but they ignore me."

Kahi agreed, adding, "You would think some of the sisters grew up in suburban-sheltered lives, but I know for a fact that they come from the same community that I did, we were all black and poor, strugglin'—but here they put on this pseudo act as if they are better."

These common concerns about relational issues on campus were summarized by Betsy, who made connections to their roots in the culture of many persons of African descent. At the end of this first session, the leaders gave each member a book which had been selected because of its relevance to their life experiences and which had been identified in the screening interviews. For this group, *Sisters of the Yam: Black Women and Self Esteem,* by bell hooks, was chosen. This book addresses healing, taking care of self, management of emotional pain and stress, and building a sense of meaning in one's life. Leaders expected that the members could relate their personal issues to these themes. Other books had also been considered, and excerpts from them were used on some occasions, although not to the same degree as *Sisters of the Yam*. The book's title referred to a support group which had been led by the author and which appeared similar to this students' group. *Yam* symbolizes a "life-sustaining system of black kinship and community."[22] Betsy read the following lines to the group:

> The power of the group to transform one another's lives seemed to be determined by the intensity of each individual's desire to recover, to find a space within and without, where she could sustain the will to be well and create affirming habits of being.[23]

After this reading, members were asked to think critically about how their lives might be connected to societal issues and the sociopolitical context in which everyone was forced to function. To get in touch with self, to understand all the factors causing one's pain, as hooks says,

> . . . means learning about the myriad ways racism, sexism, class exploitation, homophobia, and various other structures of domination operate in our daily lives to undermine our capacity to be self-determining. Without knowing what factors have created certain problems in the first place we could not begin to develop meaningful strategies of personal and collective resistance.[24]

Members were asked to read the first three chapters of the books, which would be discussed in the next weekly session.

In that next session members met and exchanged pleasantries and chatted:

"How was your week?"

"Great!"

"Not good as I had hoped, I didn't hear from my friend!"

After a few minutes, Betsy asked, "Are we ready?"

There was enthusiastic agreement. With help from the group, the leaders summarized a chapter of hooks's book, "Seeking After Truth," which discusses the importance of facing reality, no matter how painful an issue is, and becoming and remaining mentally healthy. It also examines the way in which societal process has programmed African-Americans to hide the truth, to use lies and falsehoods as mechanisms for survival. The leaders called attention to hooks's quote of the famous poet Paul Lawrence Dunbar on the important mechanism of wearing a mask as a survival mechanism:

> We wear the mask that grins and lies,
> It hides our cheeks and shades our eyes;
> This debt we pay to human guile;
> With torn and bleeding hearts we smile;
> And mouth with myriad subtleties.
> Why should the world be over-wise;
> In counting all our tears and sighs?
> Nay, let them only see us, while
> We wear the mask.[25]

bell hooks further explores the consequence:

> Encouraged to wear the mask to ensure survival in relation to the white world, black folks found themselves using strategies of dissimulation and withholding truth in interpersonal relationships within black communities. This was especially true for gender relations.[26]

Ellie associated these quotes to the burden of living on a majority campus: "I live this way. Everyday. I feel this about my life on this campus." Sensing tension, Betsy asked if she would explain how it affects her. Ellie responded:

> It's like living in two different worlds. You talk and act a certain way with blacks. You talk and act another way with whites. You go from one way to another. Sometimes it gets to me. It really bothers me.

Another member expressed her perpetual sense of discomfort and exclusion which prompted her to wonder, "Do they [white students] want us here?"

Others echoed similar feelings and concerns about belonging, being part of and at the same time apart from the dominant university culture. The discussion moved to a sentiment expressed by Tiffany: "Who cares what the other students think as long as I get a good education? That's why I'm here."

They identified the pervasive ambivalence with which they struggled; the back and forth swing, regarding whether to accept, let alone push for, greater participation and integration or whether to withdraw and turn inward to be with one's own group in campus life: clearly, for them, an agonizing question.

The leaders, especially Betsy, helped the students to expand their discussion of feelings and attitudes about being at the university. The pride taken in being good enough (read: smart enough) to get admitted and at the same time resentment associated with feeling isolated and rejected were intense contradictory responses. Wondering if they were "really wanted" and if they were thought of as "second best" had been draining emotionally and psychologically.

There were other comments about what it means to feel accepted and respected as distinct rather than merely "invited." Tanasha stated:

> I should feel happy to be here. But, sometimes I feel like I'm really here to teach the other students. Look at it, in one class I'm the only one. The others look to me to explain everything that happens about my people. Some of the stuff. Wow! blows your mind. They are racist and don't even know it. I mean the questions. Sometimes the way folk look at you—wow!

Kahi and Katrina related similar stories, particularly in relation to feeling exploited, and the tension escalated. Moving back to Tanasha's earlier point that she lived in two worlds, Betsy asked: "Is this too demanding?"

The reaction was that the expectation for change and acceptance was on them, rather than on non–students of color: How come we have to change? Accept them? What about us? Our feelings? Our way?

This discussion was fueled by the current campus climate which had been marked by increasing tension regarding race and diversity. Some white students were expressing their objections to what they perceived as an advantage held by students of color over them in terms of financial aid, housing assignments, and even admissions. These dynamics had been taking place at most major universities, forced as they were to grapple with (1) questions of access, (2) allocation of increasingly scarce financial aid, and (3) an increasingly diverse group of students who were becoming more and more vocal after years of silence. Some faculty, especially experienced older ones, were even more tense, remembering the seventies and Kent State.[27] Some newer, less experi-

enced faculty questioned the resistance of experienced faculty and administrators to deal and negotiate or even to reach out to the students.
There were also faculty who were not engaged with these concerns.
What had become clear was that faculty and staff wanted peace and
tranquillity. How to achieve that desired state was the question. Some
students showed evidence that they were growing increasingly comfortable with diversity and were able to make alliances across racial,
social-class, and gender lines. Other students took a political position,
characteristically withdrawal and self-imposed segregation, and challenging the goal of fuller participation which they believed was a
widely known campus myth anyway.

This tension and confusion had begun to spill over into the group as
members reflected on the tension in the campus environment. Some
were being confronted by schoolmates—integrate or segregate? What
should a member do? Join up with campus protesters or stay on the
sidelines? Being pulled into heated stances was beginning to consume
valuable time and energy.[28]

The group leaders, Cathy and Betsy, surfaced the issue in terms they
understood, turning these dynamics into opportunities for growth.
They underscored the value of a quality education and the danger that
members risk their chances for success by being distracted from their
educational goals and instead becoming embroiled in campus contro-
versy. They also provided guidance regarding learning to manage such
tension which, if properly handled, could be a growth experience for
the members: how to frame debates with schoolmates, take a position,
discuss points, and even argue politely and persuasively from that position. For these young women this was a new behavioral expectation,
accustomed as some were to put-downs and other provocative, even
hostile exchanges. Both leaders were well aware of the perniciousness of
intolerance. Betsy addressed this concern pointing out that many people in the university and in this country had learned how to cross
racial, class, and gender boundaries. Should they try to do likewise?
The pros and cons were discussed and sometimes these were the best
exchanges. Finally, most members agreed to try to bring ideas of flexibility and tolerance to the campus scene, but this was not unanimous.
Two members were definitely opposed, asserting that the burden of

tolerance was placed too frequently on people of African descent. And, they pointed out, the dominant group members "never" change. Betsy stepped in, asking: "Is it the case that majority people *never* change?" This caused some to pause and think. Katie commented that majority people

> . . . may change but they don't like to. Look, the university states that all are welcome but then they let you hang out there with little help. There are not enough of us to make a difference on campus. The classroom can be cold—especially if you're the only sister in the class.

On predominately white campuses where there are a small number of students of color and an even smaller number of women of African descent, comparative isolation is not unusual. In this regard students of color at many universities complain that white faculty are often insensitive and do not understand the climate (intimidation, isolation, denigration) experienced by some students, albeit not all.[29]

Language which had become heated among students on the campus also became so in the group. Students were saying unpleasant things about one another and were communicating with disrespect.

Middle Phase

By this time the group was at its midpoint. Drawing again from the literature the leaders called attention to hooks's chapter "Tongues of Fire," on how the use of language contributes to the development of attitudes that we share about one another. The chapter explores how telling the truth, which has constituted a way of coping with painful reality and undoing the destructiveness of the learned responses of denial and lying, can be an effective coping tool but can also become a weapon. An excerpt was read:

> What we all participated in was a practice of verbal assault, truth telling as a weapon. . . . This practice often takes the form of calling somebody out, that is "reading" them, or in a milder form "dissing" them. . . . It usually takes place in a context where the intent is to hurt or wound.[30]

The discussion centered on how telling the truth can slip into negative language and put-downs, which appear to be common behaviors among some African Americans. bell hooks goes on to note that language put-downs are behaviors learned early on in the home:

> Harsh criticism, with a truth telling component, is often a major characteristic of black mother and daughter relationship.[31]

hooks traces the use of this behavior to survival strategies developed in order to manage in a "white supremacist context."[32]

In the very first session, Tanasha had raised concerns about relationships among the students on the campus, specifically "the put-downs, scorn, and hate." Linking this sentiment to hooks, the following passage was reviewed:

> We need to better understand how black folks who feel relatively powerless to control their destiny exercise negative power over one another in hierarchical settings.[33]

The emphatic response of members to this reading was a measure of their engagement, even excitement, with the topic and their willingness to participate. At that point in the process, members felt safe to pursue this subject because the focus was on the literature, not their personal "problems." As members felt more secure, this would change and they would relate their own experiences back to the literature, thinking and connecting their issues to bell hooks's artistry.

In response to this reading, Tanasha, who had spoken up initially, wanted to expand on her comment about how students were treated on a majority campus. Her comment revealed how negatives in the campus environment can spill over into personal relationships. She explained how she had reached out to her Latina roomate to bring her into the group. Their problems arose from the fact that neither knew how to recognize and then externalize their anger about how they were being treated on a campus that they perceived as racist. The conflict had grown, becoming so heated on the part of one that she was deemed not ready for the group because she had such poor control over her anger. A complicating factor had been that Tanasha perceived her Latina roommate, when with her Latina friends, to distance from her, acting as though they were "not friends, just roommates."

In the group the leaders approached the anger issue from both personal and societal perspectives. Not only did they place it in the context of members' experiences with racism but in the context of their belonging to different cultures which group members then discussed. The leaders asked Tanasha to explore what might be the motivation for such behavior: misunderstanding due to (1) different expectations about friends and communication among friends, and (2) differing cultural expectations about how much to invest in a relationship/friendship.

Processing members' anger about racism on the campus also surfaced the issue of the paucity of black men for dates. This issue was crystallized when Tiffany made a curious remark: "Black people can't have sex on this campus because of all the tension."

When this issue was clarified, it turned out that Tiffany was expressing her belief that the stresses resulting from their treatment on campus were interfering with the capacity for close relationships between the males and females. Moreover, the paucity of black males was being compounded by the fact that some of them were dating non-black women. The leaders directed the discussion to three points: that sex can never be the key to developing relationships anywhere, including on campus; members might consider the option of developing relationships with persons other than just black males, and members might consider opportunities to become acquainted with males on other college and university campuses.

The group then focused on ways of getting to know males and how to develop appropriate and respectful relationships with males and females. As a result, one member developed and executed a forum on black male-female relationships which was well attended, providing further opportunity for dialogue, exchange of views, and personal growth. Embodying traditional gender concerns black male-female relationships are burdened also by societal dynamics such as the constrained opportunity structure that has plagued African Americans during and since slavery. Another significant factor is that black males have been even more trapped in stereotypes than females. One reason the women's discussion was so painful was that the group was dealing with such intractable societal stereotypes as "male stud," "sex-craved females." But dealing with this issue as they did enhanced trust within the group, which in turn facilitated greater disclosure and ultimately member growth.[34]

Modeling and Mirroring

The group also helped members learn to confront other forms of racism and to manage their responses.[35] For example, they discussed incidents in which they perceived a professor as behaving in a racist manner. The leaders cautioned group members about the danger of using "the perception of racism as a crutch." As one leader put it: "Whether or not the professor was racist must not be allowed to keep you from sticking to your goals." Techniques were discussed relating to managing the experience of being distanced from or made invisible by professors. One suggested response was to be persistent in communicating with them ("be in their offices every week"), which members interpreted to mean "being in their faces." Suggested the leader:

> The more uncomfortable you feel, the more questions you should be asking, and the more you should seek interaction with them [the professors].

From time to time the practitioner reflected back to the group member how she, as a student, was coming across to the professor; when the behavior was offputting all members could observe it and understand the need for direct, nonhostile interaction. Using the techniques of mirroring and modeling, the leader shared her personal experience with specific problems under discussion to show that she had been in the same situation and how she "got unstuck." For example, in relation to the discussion on black men, the leader reassured the members:

> I had the same experience and even now am still having it. There just are not a lot of black males to choose from. This does not change when you get older. What must change is the commitment to self—to focus on one's goals and where one seeks to go.

Personal issues do impact the work of the leader, as hard as one might try to retain objectivity. Reid comments: "No matter how hard we, as group leaders, try to separate our professional life from our personal life, it is difficult if not impossible to keep the two apart."[36] Like the group member the group leader brings to the helping situation a multitude of life experiences that impact on the therapeutic relationship. It is the worker's humanness that provides a basis for his or her relating to the members. However, this same humanness can be destructive and an impediment to change.[37]

In the example above, one of the leaders attempted to help members understand and cope with the sociological reality that more black males are in prison than in college,[38] limiting the supply of upwardly mobile male companions. In this case, the leaders did not consider suggesting that students develop contacts and relationships with non-college black men (blue-collar workers), which has been a solution resorted to by black women for generations.[39]

Final Phase

Reviewing their progress, there was agreement among the members that they had learned to appreciate and applaud Betsy's message on tolerance. The women reached a new realization of its desirability and their capacity of becoming bicultural and living in a bicultural environment, and they wanted to become role models for others. They agreed to stop using put-down language; now understanding how devastating it can be to others. They would not put down other people of African descent and they would, indeed, refuse to use put-down language against anyone. Furthermore they would confront others who used put-down language in their presence. Discovering the admiration and respect they had for one another they planned to turn to one another with questions on topics ranging from computers to financial aid. Indeed the group became a positive force in campus life, although there were some (non-group) students of African descent who felt they sold out by embracing and exhibiting tolerance on issues relating to diversity.

Finally, we note that in the beginning, literature was used to help free up members to identify and discuss strong, emotionally painful issues. By the middle sessions the group needed no such props. They had now learned that the group provided an adequate safety zone for sharing, exchanging, and confronting ideas and problems. This innovative approach worked well for these motivated, articulate college women.

Outcomes

There were no dropouts in this group and sessions were well attended. In terms of specific behavioral outcomes, in addition to the positives noted above, the following were observable: better grades, increased ability to problem solve, the formation of new friendships and the resolution of conflict that had prevented positive relationships, use of networking, and the mentoring of younger students.

A GROUP FOR WELL CHILDREN IN HIV/AIDS AFFECTED FAMILIES

Though their life situation may be precarious since they are at high risk of being orphaned, little is known about the children of HIV/AIDS victims. The number of children so affected has grown along with the increase in persons with the disease, particularly among those who are poor and of color. It was estimated that by 1995, 45,000 children and adolescents would be orphans because of the disease.[40]

Children living with an HIV/AIDS parent must cope with great uncertainty. They live from day to day not knowing the health status of the parent. Some children carry the responsibility of caregiver, having to minister to the sick parent. They become exposed to adult troubles, never having the luxury of being a child or enjoying childhood. The burdens these children are forced to shoulder in the home are compounded by the stigma they carry outside in the world. Despite the fact that death is a concept many children do not even comprehend, these children are forced to face the possibility of loss every day. Some, of course, try to avoid the issue. Having to confront the loss of a parent or another close relative compounds the developmental process, particularly in relation to questions of dependence upon parents or other adults.[41] These children, as a result, end up experiencing loss and bereavement prior to their actual occurrence. Some are also frightened of contracting the disease and of dying themselves.[42] Such burdens take a high psychological and physical toll. Confused, tired, angry, and threatened, these young people act out in ways that are often destructive to themselves and/or others.

As tragic as this scenario is, it is even bleaker for children of color who face additional stressors because of societal abuse: poverty, homelessness, unsafe neighborhoods and deprived physical environments, as well as personal abuse—physical, sexual, emotional, and mental.[43]

Purpose and Formation

This discussion explores a group intervention approach for children from HIV/AIDS or seropositive families. A community needs assessment had determined that these children were falling through the cracks in the helping system structures since social agencies and other organizations were focusing on providing assistance to persons who were actually infected with HIV/AIDS or on preventing the spread of the HIV infection.

Contracting for Goals

The general goals of the group were to provide to these children the necessary psycho-educational and other resource supports. Individual and family therapy were made available to augment group work when necessary.

A major goal for leaders was to help the group agree to focus on issues of safety, assisting the children to think about ways to take care of themselves and choose safer ways of behaving. This was particularly necessary since they dealt with their fears about their caretakers' health and their own health with behavior characterized by poor judgment, engagement in unprotected sex, substance abuse, and out-of-control behavior (for adolescents) and general acting out (for latency age children). The experiences shared below focus mostly on the adolescent group, with one example taken from the group of younger children.

Recruitment and Screening

Children were referred by parents, teachers, and providers. To be eligible for membership in the group, one of their family members had to have HIV or AIDS. At a prescreening interview with both parent and child, information was given about the group and how the prospective member might benefit from the experience. Also discussed were the expectations of the parent and child, concerns about disclosure, and fears about belonging to a group. Before signing on, a child was permitted to attend three group meetings at which time a focused effort was made to build a strong relationship with both parent and child.

Potential members were expected to make a commitment to participate fully and to respect confidentiality. Respect and confidentiality involved a recognition that safety in relation to self and others would not be sacrificed. This was of central importance because of the children's tendency to manage their fears related to HIV/AIDS by engaging in destructive, violent behaviors.

Group Composition

Two groups were formed, one for latency children, aged 8 to 10 years, and one for adolescents aged 13 to 17 years. Of the 17 children in both groups, 14 were receiving public assistance. Four were caucasian, eight were African-American, and five were multiracial (as distinct from biracial). AIDS had affected these children variously: two had lost parents and continued to have other family members who were affected; three were in foster care because their parents who were too ill to care for them; four were cared for by grandparents; six lived with mother only; two lived with mother and a sibling both of whom had AIDS.

WOMEN AND CHILDREN'S GROUPS

Early Phase

Since the group was open-ended and new members continued to join up, these early sessions for any given individual were focused on including him or her as a group member. When a new member joined the group, introductions were made through a "go round" so that personal information on all members would be known. This information related to each member's age, favorite food and pastime, school grade, and teacher. Also discussed was the member's assessment of past experiences, if any, with groups and the reasons for coming to this one.

Discussion was initiated at each weekly session by the use of a special technique. The members were asked to rate their week (1 = terrible; 10 = terrific). The rating opened up the discussion for all the members and gave them the latitude to respond in some specific manner to the changes within the family and/or within themselves. In the early group sessions, and again when new members were added to the group, group leaders facilitated some discussion about HIV and AIDS basics, addressing each member's feelings about the illness.

Mid to Later Phase

As members became more relaxed in later sessions, they more readily opened up, discussing more freely their concerns and feelings in relation to themselves and family members. They were able to bring out in the open their sense of betrayal and pain about the "family secret." Often members' opening up led to a teaching moment which permitted the practitioners to provide information about resources available to members and their families. As the group progressed, a strong alliance was built around their shared problem. This was observable early on and became the basis for a healthy, mutually supportive environment. The group became like an extended family, where concerns were shared and empathy extended to one another.

All was not sadness though. Young people can be very resilient, which was often manifest in their humor and creativity. For example:

Ron, a 14-year-old whose mother had AIDS and whose sister was born seronegative, periodically brought in some rap music which he sang to the rest of the group. His spontaneity and creative ability gave group members something to look forward to each week. It also opened up more sharing of the children's gifts with each other.

Julie, a 15-year-old, had great writing skills and on two occasions brought in poems she had composed. Her dream to be a writer was kept alive within the group even as her ailing father, who had abused her as a younger child, was now dying of AIDS. Although her poems had a depressive tone to them, Julie was determined to become a writer and this was clearly evident in the redemptive quality with which she often concluded her poems.

Tara, a 17-year-old, and Judy, a 14-year-old, shared pictures of their families with the group. One session was spent sharing stories about those caretakers whose pictures they brought and who were now at the brink of death.

While group process is never smooth or linear and this one was no different, it was marked by an escalation in destructive and intolerant behavior which was closely associated with the progressive nonyielding symptomatology of stricken family members. Such behavior grew out of the children's very real sense of depression, fear, and confusion. For example:

Wayne, a 13-year-old, had a history of a head injury that had occurred at age two. His father, heavily involved in drugs, had been in and out of jail and was now diagnosed with HIV. His teachers reported out-of-control behavior. Wayne was disruptive in the classroom and he had been moved from school to school, leaving the school administration frustrated. His mother, with five other children, was overwhelmed by guilt and the lack of support within the home. Wayne's response was a determination to be "invincible." This invincibility was evidenced in his recklessness about safe sex and other safety issues. As an adolescent, Wayne tended to rebel, act out, and to display an "illusion of invulnerability." He was also driven to take on a parental role with his younger siblings in the absence of a responsible caretaker and was in search of the zeal his father had displayed before getting involved in drugs. Wayne's behavior showed a child who was going through major and multiple loss traumas. His hopes to be reunited with his father after each jail term were cut short by reincarceration. His internal isolation was acted out in external isolation as he involved himself in negative, destructive, and self-destructive behaviors.

Wayne handled his painful situation through the use of power-over behavior and carelessness, behaviors frequently engaged in as a response to vulnerability and entrapment in powerless societal roles.[44] Wayne was offered an opportunity to act out his coping strategy within the structure of the group and with the attention of skillful practitioners. When his behavior was recognized for what it was, an attempt to be strong and courageous in the face of terror, he could be directed away from acting out in ways that were harmful for others and to their property. Thus he and the community benefited.

Techniques

The group's co-leaders, always holding the members to high expectations,[45] established a code of "responsible truth-saying," defined as helping members face the reality of their painful situation. Such expectations meant that group members would be able to marshal their strength to undo their denial, to face their grief, to manage and redirect their anger, and not become overwhelmed and immobilized by their extreme realities.

The techniques used in this group model included story telling, externalization, instruction, modeling, role playing, planning along with restructuring, and letter writing.[46] In using the story-telling technique, each child was encouraged to relate his or her experience in a way that was comfortable to the storyteller. Although this activity mobilized some fear for the storytellers, the children later acknowledged its usefulness in terms of how much they learned. In reflecting on their own experiences, story telling allowed the children to expand on their own stories as well as those of group members. Paintings, artwork, and rap music which they themselves created amplified the story telling. To support expression of positives in their lives, children were asked to share at least one humorous moment in their daily activities.

In using externalization, the leaders encouraged the younger children to represent in figures, symbols, or metaphors the out-of-control impulses and self-destructive behaviors they were unable to control, which could then be addressed in a constructive way. For example, a figure called "Mr. Monster" was proposed as one who caused bad things to happen to good people who then experienced dangerous and frightening moments. The children were encouraged to dialogue with "Mr. Monster" in order to drive him away. As a result they could feel some control in their lives. While identifying "Mr. Monster" in their lives did not come easily for some, they understood better their personal sense of powerlessness and lack of control and developed a new readiness to do battle with "Mr. Monster." A variety of names were also used to humanize other negative forces that were present in the children's lives which permitted the children to talk through their problems and anxieties.

Additional techniques used by the leaders to teach members new behaviors included instruction, modeling, role playing, and restructuring. For example, one leader reported:

*On one occasion, **Wayne** described in great detail how he stole a bike. I remember going over the incident with him asking him to identify different feelings and thoughts that were going on for him at each of the moments he had so proudly discussed with the group. It was clear that he had not thought about the connection between the feelings and behaviors prior to stealing the bike. My focus, and eventually, the focus of some of the members, was to help Wayne identify the "triggers" that led him to do such things. The "triggers" were often people, places, feelings, and situations. Identifying alternative behaviors and learning to restructure thought processes were key to doing this. For Wayne, three words captured what we were about: "think before acting."*

Encouraging the children to participate in planning activities and to help set the direction of the group increased their sense of control, responsibility, and commitment.

Letter writing is used in intervention to help clients express uncomfortable feelings. It was used to encourage the children to express the pain and ambivalence they felt toward all members of their families. They wrote letters, which were not actually delivered, not only to family members who were living but also to those who had died. The children "did report that they felt good about writing these letters."

Outcomes

This group model facilitated members' sense of belonging, being accepted and cared for. Members also learned useful survival skills particularly in the areas of managing anger, controlling impulses and solving problems, and having safer sex. Tara's experience is an example of effective outcome.

> *Tara is a 17-year-old girl. She was referred to the group by her 24-year-old sister who was concerned about Tara's isolation and anger which she often acted out in explosive and impulsive ways. Tara's mother was dying of AIDS. Her mother had separated from her father when Tara was about four years old. Apparently, as a child she was shuffled between both parents, and her father, who had remarried, won custody of Tara when she was 12. This was when Tara's oppositional behavior toward her father began. Shortly thereafter, Tara learned about her mother's drug habit and her contracting HIV. Tara began having difficulties in school, skipping school, and running away from home. When Tara first came to the group, she was very reserved and skeptical about the whole experience. Once in the group, she heard other children talk about their difficulties and immediately found a connection with other kids. Later, she said: "I thought I was going to be the worst." What helped her was developing the ability to link her behavior to feelings associated with her mother's illness. At one point she ran away from home and lived with a friend for two weeks. During those two weeks while her father had reported her missing, Tara continued to come to the support group. Later she stated: "It was the one place that no one would judge me." It is evident she felt a sense of safety, connection, and kinship within the group, which offered something cathartic for her.*

Earlier we cited goals identified by the co-leaders. As a result of the group process, the participants achieved the following outcomes:

- They developed and maintained a sense of connectedness and mutual support.
- They confronted and reduced their fear, anger, and confusion via the provision of a supportive environment. This was manifest in their improved capacity for anger management.
- They learned to recognize and express their sadness appropriately as manifested in less aggressive behavior toward self and community.

- They developed a sense of extended family who could be counted on for support in times of trouble.
- They increased academic and social competence, self-esteem and self development.

Tara, Wayne, Ron, and Julie were examples from the 17 participants who benefited from this intervention.

Practitioners Sharing Leadership

In the three vignettes—Women Saving Face, University Women of African Descent, and Well Children in HIV/AIDS Affected Families—groups were facilitated by the use of co-therapists. Also, one group used the services of a translator. Co-therapists bring additional resources to the group process, particularly in relation to scheduling, because one can be present if the other is absent. More than one leader also means additional resources for members since two practitioners can offer expanded theoretical capabilities and the presence of additional skills, values, and feelings, all of which increase chances for success. For example, at times one therapist may take an active and instrumental role while the other observes, listens, takes notes, and plays a key role in the postgroup debriefing that co-practitioners usually engage in. After each meeting the leaders would meet to evaluate the session and plan next steps. Consideration would be given to whether the theme of the session needed to be continued the next week either because of its significance to the members or because more discussion was needed. If a member became upset as a result of the discussion, crying for example, the leaders would consider whether or not to contact the member during the week to offer additional support. If a member failed to show, a follow-up would determine what caused the absence. In the children's groups, one co-therapist might hold and comfort a child who manifested sadness, camouflaged though it might be as aggressive acting out—such as swearing, kicking, and yelling—while the other might continue with the group in the instrumental leader role. When the child became calm enough, the leader could help him or her move back into the session as a more participatory member. Two agencies and one university allocated the necessary resources that permitted the use of co-therapists in these groups.

When translators are used, additional challenges and opportunities are posed. Earlier, the additional clock time involved in such groups was noted as well as the way in which the process is affected. What must also be added is concern for the impact of managed care on both co-led groups and groups requiring the use of a translator. In the managed care accountability environment now so characteristic of social service delivery, there is little appreciation of how much clock time translator-assisted groups and co-led groups require. Important as this work is, agencies are hard pressed to secure funding to support such critical strategies.

6

MIXED GROUPS
Vignettes

INTRODUCTION

By way of contrast and to illustrate the differences that may often occur in work with clients who occupy differing power roles in the social system, we offer this examination of practitioner work with two mixed-gender groups: the Long-Term Recovery group, whose participants were white middle- and upper-class, and a working-class Black-Hispanic parent education/growth group. Brief though they are, these two vignettes capture dynamics that show differences in process due to gender and social class factors.

The sobriety group participants ranged in age from 25 to 55. The problems they brought did not appear to be as connected to larger societal systemic processes as did those of the black-Hispanic group. They had no economic trials compounded by joblessness, dangerous neighborhoods, gangs, and racism. These clients possessed resources, could function on jobs, and could purchase mental health services to combat alcoholism. They were, nonetheless, also overwhelmed and in need of help and supportive services. Despite rising crime rates in suburban

areas, these participants were not personally exposed to criminal violence. This group is included here because it demonstrates (1) the
salience of economic sufficiency and what money can buy—that is,
good long-term clinical service delivered in a safe therapeutic environment at a distinguished mental health facility, and (2) the difference in
group process when context (social class and racism) is not an issue that
members must struggle with.

AN ALCOHOL-SOBRIETY GROUP

Purpose and Formation

The overarching purpose of this ongoing co-led group is to help members maintain long-term sobriety from alcohol and drugs and to assist
them in achieving and maintaining the highest level of functioning.
The group was developed to provide a resource for supporting long-
term sobriety for clients who had recently completed a detox program.
While client attendance varies, the average length of time in the group
is three years. Among current members, attendance has ranged from
six months to twelve years. Both the leaders and the participants have
been male and female. All are caucasian.

Goals and Rules

The goals of the group are to:

- Understand the dynamics of alcoholism
- Understand the stressors that mobilize drinking behavior
- Understand the connection between one's need for alcohol and af-
  fective responses that one experiences, such as anxiety, pain, shame,
  anger
- Develop alternatives to substance abuse as a coping behavior
- Provide support for maintaining sobriety

This group, like most, established rules to live by. These included
maintaining confidentiality, and agreement that issues stemming from
any outside contact between group members during regular attendance must be brought into the group for discussion.

Group Compostion

The group consisted of six members aged 25 to 55, two women and four men. Four had an attachment to the labor force, and two were full-time graduate students.

Beth A. *was a 42-year-old married mother of three who was currently enrolled in a full-time graduate counseling program in a local university. She presented as an attractive, well-dressed woman whose participation in group alternated between active advocacy, nurturance of other group members, and a sharp-tongued, critical attitude toward them. She had a twenty-year history of alcohol and valium abuse which led her to seek inpatient treatment, from which she subsequently was referred to the Long-Term Recovery group. Along with stresses associated with her new sobriety and attendance at graduate school, she was having difficulty in her relationship with her husband.*

Al B. *was a 38-year-old single, gay male who worked part-time in a hair salon. He presented as a somewhat overweight man, who was pleasant and friendly in his demeanor. Approximately ten years earlier, Mr. B. had suffered a serious brain injury in a boating accident which limited his cognitive functioning. Prior to this, Mr. B. had been an aspiring artist who was attending graduate school on a full scholarship. His long history of alcohol abuse became worse following the accident. At the time of our contact with the group leaders he was having a difficult time maintaining sobriety, which generally manifested itself in drinking slips in which he drank alone in his bedroom.*

Don C. *was a 39-year-old divorced male who was currently living alone while attending graduate school, where he was studying structural engineering. A tall slender man who wore a distinctive handlebar mustache and cowboy boots, his characteristic manner of interacting was direct and, at times, angry. He had a long-term history of alcohol abuse which had escalated during his unsuccessful marriage and had continued to plague him as he tried to manage the requirements of graduate school.*

Carla D. *was a 46-year-old single, lesbian woman who was employed at a marine supply store, and who lived with her partner and two* cats. *She presented as a healthy middle-aged woman, wearing short hair, casual baggy clothes, appearing and acting younger than her stated age. She tended to be somewhat quiet and careful in her manner of relating, seeming not to want to divulge too much information too quickly. She had had a long history of experimenting with drugs dating back to the 1960s, but was currently struggling with an alcohol problem. Her other significant problem involved her relationship with her partner.*

Frank E. was a 55-year-old state employee who was married with four children. Generally disheveled in appearance, often wearing gym shorts and sweatshirts, he presented an anti-authoritarian attitude, and saw himself as a voice for underprivileged people. In the group he was an active member, very giving and supportive to others. An abuser of alcohol for most of his life, he had returned to treatment following five years of sobriety which had ended when he became seriously depressed and resumed drinking.

Elmer F. was a 49-year-old single researcher who lived alone. Mr. F. appeared and acted older than his stated age. He came to group meetings wearing his company's name tag on the lapel of his suit jacket. He presented in a friendly, polite manner, but was a self-described loner who was somewhat rigid. He socialized very little, and spent most of his vacation time with his mother in the South. He had had a long history of alcohol abuse, having referred himself to treatment when he had begun drinking at his desk at work and feared that he might lose his job. Along with his alcohol problem, he got very anxious about his management duties at work where he was director of a research division which included 95 scientists.

Group Process

The dynamics reviewed here represent only a snapshot of this open-ended group which has been in existence for 17 years and is expected to continue as participants enter and terminate in an ongoing fashion. Our practitioner-informant had co-led the group throughout its 17-year history.

Consistent with the focus on maintaining sobriety, members were encouraged ". . . to discuss potential stressors that might trigger a drinking or drug slip, identifying alternative coping strategies to deal with these potential relapse situations, and thoroughly analyzing the feelings and behavior around an actual 'slip.' The group leader employs a basic psycho-dynamic approach which encourages members to seek awareness of unconsciously driven behaviors along with problem-solving, psycho-educational, and supportive therapy approaches."[1]

Real change is conceptualized by the leader as resulting from group processes marked by significant interaction between members or between a member and the leader(s). These interactions are viewed as creating opportunity for understanding the self and for becoming cognizant of internal psychological processes (thoughts, beliefs, and behavioral tendencies) that usually lie outside of awareness. Acquiring such awareness is believed to result in greater clarity of experiences, feelings, and perspectives that are connected with the need for alcohol.

Examples of opportunities for learning about self through interacting with others include these incidents between Beth and Al.

Beth A. had been in group for approximately one year when Al B. entered the group. Al appeared different from other group members in that a brain injury which he had suffered years earlier had produced cognitive impairment as manifest in his seriously diminished attention span and prompt use of circumstantial thought processes. His attitude was very friendly and outgoing as he seemed to crave human contact and friendship with other group members. About three weeks after Al started in the group, Beth telephoned the male co-leader between group sessions. She was upset that the leaders had brought into the group a member who was "beneath the group's intellectual capacity." She questioned their judgment, explaining that she did not feel that Al was capable of keeping group information confidential, and demanded that he be assigned to a group for brain-injured patients. The leader responded that these issues would have to be taken up in group. In the next group session, when Beth failed to raise the issue of her concerns about Al, the therapist revealed that he had received a phone call from her during the preceding week. Beth interrupted and in an irritated voice said that she could not believe that the therapist was raising this issue in Al's presence. She then attempted to state, in as careful a manner as possible, her concerns about whether Al "belonged" in this group. Al defensively responded that he did not want to be part of a group that did not want him, and was visibly shaken—both angry and sad. Most of the group supported Al, and expressed their commitment to having him remain in the group.

Exploration of this interaction led to the surfacing of significant issues for each of them: Al's inability to cope with people's response to him and Beth's ambivalence about men. One of the primary determinants of the destructive drinking behavior Al engaged in following his accident was that he no longer felt that he fit in anywhere. Fully cognizant of his diminished cognitive capacity, he felt different from others and he was excruciatingly lonely as a result. To have had this issue exposed so directly for the entire group to deal with provided Al with an opportunity to address an issue that had been causing him much pain. To cope effectively it was necessary for him to confront the reality of his situation—that is, the reality of other people's distancing and even rejection reactions toward him, and to develop some means of coping with this pain other than drinking. For Beth, what emerged was her disdain for weak, ineffectual men. Her mother had been an aggressive, domineering woman from whom Beth had distanced, seeking solace from her father. However, her father avoided both mother and daughter by escaping into alcohol, causing Beth much embarrassment throughout her childhood. As a result she had developed a "double-barreled" reaction to all men (including her husband) who did not portray themselves in a masculine, forthright, and decisive manner. For Al, Beth epitomized all of the intolerant people in his life that had caused him so much heartache; and for Beth, Al represented the handicapped, ineffectual father who had let her down so often in her childhood. The two continued in group, learning much about themselves from knowing each other.

This next vignette involves the interaction between a group member and the group therapist. Don C. had attended the group for approximately six weeks when the following interaction took place. Sometime during the first half hour of the group, Don asked the group leaders exactly what their role was in the group.

He was told that what he had observed during the previous five weeks was typical of the way in which therapists operated—that is, their role was basically that of facilitating group discussion. Other group members were asked their opinions of the leader's role and of members' participation, and a general discussion ensued. Don seemed unsatisfied with their responses and demanded that the leaders answer the question directly. His remarks were particularly aimed at the male co-leader. Again an attempt was made to offer some minimal explanation, and to suggest that since he had already observed for himself the group process, he was now encouraged to express any dissatisfaction he was feeling about how the leaders were conducting the group. Again he demanded an explicit answer, for which there was none forthcoming from the leader. At this point, Don abruptly stormed out of the room, slamming the door behind him.

Fortunately, the next week Don returned to the group, which gave an opportunity to process what had happened. He voiced his anger and frustration at the male co-leader for failing to give him the information that he wanted and felt entitled to. He was assured that his frustration was understandable and that his anger was justifiable; however, what was questioned was the extent of his reaction. And when he was asked about others in his life who had failed him, it became immediately apparent that his relationship with his father had been tumultuous. Don described his father as a coldhearted, overly critical man whom he had tried to please all of his life. His anger at the male co-leader had been typical of his explosive reactions to males he perceived as frustrating. In the course of this discussion he acknowledged that he had also had difficulty with a number of male professors at the university over the years, and that one of the major issues confronting him in the present had been his conflictual relationship with the chairperson of his graduate thesis committee. This conflict had gotten to the point that he was now in jeopardy of not completing the program. With the help of the group, he became more skilled in recognizing his intense reactions to authoritarian males, and able to analyze his reactions in a rational manner. Two years later, as Don was successfully completing his graduate thesis, he smiled as he remarked that the group leader had still not answered his question, and that he was grateful.

A PARENT EDUCATION/GROWTH GROUP

Purpose and Formation

The aim of this mixed black and Hispanic parent group is to help members improve their child management skills and capabilities. This group vignette demonstrates that even a small group of three can offer a chance for growth and that a mixed-gender group may offer a male single parent unique opportunities in that regard. The group, which was short-term (ten weeks), was unique in that the children of the parent group members were involved in a simultaneously run children's group. Though this discussion examines some data from the children's group, it focuses on the parents' group, showing how the practitioners helped the parents to think through problems that interfered with effective child management, including relationship and reality problems.

Goals and Rules

The goals of the group were to:

- Expose members to basic knowledge on child development and child care
- Help members improve parenting skills
- Connect members to community helping resources

All participants had received other services from the agency and had been referred by an agency staff member.

Rules governing the group were established by the members with strong assistance from the leader. These centered on prompt meeting attendance, maintaining confidentiality, and behaving toward one another with respect. Members were aware that each of them had one or more children who were receiving services from the agency and who were participating in the children's group. All were single parents.

Group Composition

Holliman was a 38-year-old African-American male, father of a bright, energetic five-year-old girl, Tashi, whose custody he had gained two years earlier, in 1995, because her mother had been arrested and convicted for possessing and selling drugs. Although Holliman had had a relationship with his daughter prior to gaining custody of her, he was not familiar with the tasks of her daily care and had made no plans in this regard. In fact, he had not thought very much about the demands of parenting. Complicating his new role as custodial parent was the fact that Holliman was living with his mother, who was displeased to learn that her son wished to help his daughter by taking on the role of active parent and planned to bring the child into the home where they lived.

In addition to the stressor of an actively unsupportive mother, this young father struggling to be responsible for his child was laid off from his job soon after his daughter arrived to live with him. Anxious then also about money and loss of the health benefits that had been offered by his employer, he found the demands of coping with his mother's behavior as he sought to raise his child increasingly discouraging and undermining.

Proud and determined, Holliman found the possibility of having to accept welfare—which the agency encouraged him to accept while continuing his search for a job—untenable. While the search was not initially productive and took a long time, Holliman did eventually find employment. However, the company was moving to downsize, and Holliman, as the "last hired, first fired," was soon out of work. Now welfare was his only option, particularly because he needed to have health benefits as well as financial assistance.

Holliman's goal in the group was to become comfortable and skilled in his role as caretaker.

Thelma was a 33-year-old African-American mother of two children, a boy and a girl, who had been in an abusive relationship with Fred, the children's father, who was also her husband. After they separated, Fred refused financial support for the family and their abusive relationship continued. Afraid of what his absence from the scene might mean for the children, Thelma allowed him to visit. When he did, he often tried to force Thelma into having sex, which she despised but nonetheless felt helpless to handle, feeling frightened that if she fought him off and did not succumb to his wishes, he would stop visiting the children or even abandon them. Thelma's goals were to become more assertive, leave this miserable situation, improve her parenting skills, and get support for the children while going through the break-up.

Vivi was a 40-year-old Latino mother of three, a boy and a girl ages 17 and 15 respectively, and a younger 9-year-old boy. When their father had become abusive prior to the birth of E, the youngest child, she had left him. E had developed very serious emotional problems which Vivi was struggling to manage in the home. Her goals were to become more effective in dealing with E's problems and to generally improve her parenting skills.

The Children and Their Group

While the parents were meeting, their children were also participating in a group whose goals were to alter problem behaviors such as acting out and poor management of feelings and to learn effective social skills. The children of Holliman, Vivi, and Thelma were admitted to the group, so that they might each receive help in these areas.

Tashi, Holliman's daughter, although expressive and bright, was experiencing adjustment problems in school. Holliman received frequent calls about her behavior from school administrators. Goals for Tashi included addressing these adjustment problems and improving social skills.

David, age seven, and Eve, age six, Thelma's children, were having serious emotional difficulties. As noted earlier, the father's sexual abuse of their mother was a problem. A major concern was that David, on more than one occasion, had witnessed his parents in the sexual act, and he had no way of processing this traumatic experience. David was now having problems in school because of attention deficits, and was evaluated as suffering from ADD (Attention Deficit Disorder) and PTD (Post Traumatic Stress Disorder) stemming from his firsthand knowledge of his father's abuse of his mother.

Eve was a whiny child and Thelma would give in to her demands, probably out of exhaustion. Whatever the reason, David believed that mom favored his sister and was intimidated by Eve though she was a year younger and physically smaller. There was some unclarity about how Thelma handled the problems between Eve and David—the impression was that she was exceedingly passive, having given up parental authority. Goals for David and Eve included addressing relational issues between them and helping to resolve family conflicts. Both children needed to address behavioral problems and social skills.

José, Vivi's nine-year-old third grade boy, had serious troubles: as evidenced by smearing feces at home, impulsive behavior, and difficulty relating to other children. To say the least, it was hard for his mother and teachers to help manage him in a constructive way. These serious emotional problems were being addressed in individual therapy which had been arranged by the agency. Within the group, personal goals for José included helping him to develop more appropriate social skills.

Group Process

These vignettes describe (1) the supportive group process which enhanced knowledge about child management while also facilitating growth in parents and (2) some of the issues members dealt with and how the leader helped them think through alternatives.

Holliman's growth was achieved via his discussion of three themes: his interactions with his daughter, his interactions with his mother, and his sense of entrapment in finding alternative housing.

He expressed utter exasperation with his bright and energetic daughter, Tashi. Having little conception of the time and thought required to care for the child, Holliman announced that he had to figure out a way to care for Tashi before and after school. The agency had intervened and assisted in getting Tashi into Head Start so that she could have a structured preschool educational activity. But allowing Tashi to attend Head Start created other difficulties, since her grandmother was not supportive of the child being in her house and when she was alone with Tashi, after Holliman left for work, she abused the child. Because Holliman could not think of alternatives he was often late for work waiting for the Head Start pickup, a probable factor in Holliman's losing his job.

Using a problem-solving approach, the group leaders, along with Vivi and Thelma, challenged Holliman to consider ways of working out the conflict with his mother, presenting alternative approaches for interacting with her. When Holliman seemed unable to change his mother's confusing, undermining, and abusive behavior, they encouraged him to move out and consider family and friends who could help him. But Holliman appeared stuck and unable to leave despite the unhealthy relationship with his mother. Worried, unemployed, and with little savings, he pondered, where could he go.

When the practitioner suggested that he consider public or subsidized housing, group members familiar with this option shared their experiences reinforcing the reality that this was seemingly his last option.

In yet another exchange in the group, Holliman complained about Tashi and how stubborn she could be. "She doesn't do what I tell her," he sighed as he described the following incident:

> School had closed early because of inclement weather. Tashi was scheduled to go to a baby-sitter's home after day care but while passing her own home she noticed that her father's car was on the street. Instead of going to the baby-sitter's, she walked back to her house hoping to see her dad. When no one answered she went back to the sitter's home and played with children there, which had been the original plan. When he found out what she had done, Holliman, frightened that she could have met danger, screamed at her, calling her "bad."

Vivi and Thelma, upon hearing the story, did not see Tashi as bad or disobedient. Although they empathized with Holliman's fear for his daughter's safety, they thought the story illustrated that Tashi was smart and spunky. They pointed out that he should praise Tashi for being smart and wanting to be with her dad and that he should not badger and scream. When the leader suggested that he might have shown his approval by hugging her, they became engaged in a discussion about the need for warmth and warm feelings, especially for children. Vivi and Thelma actively encouraged Holliman to pick Tashi up and hug her. Vivi added several times emphatically. "Do it over and over." Both women pointed out that this was important particularly because the little girl was not receiving any affection from her grandmother.

Assuming that Holliman had been using the same child-rearing approaches that his mother had used, the practitioner turned this discussion into a teaching moment by moving the discussion to what the members had learned from their own childhood about how to handle specific problems with children. Gently, she asked: "Holliman, can you tell us something about how your parents brought you up?" His responses indicated that the practitioner's assumption was correct. This discussion also held significance for Thelma and Vivi, who recalled their own upbringing. Though the two women were from different cultures, African-American and Latino, they both had experienced similar harsh discipline from elders who were negative and highly critical. This discussion helped Holliman to expand his repertoire of responses to Tashi: to become readier to show her affection, to be able to offer praise for good behavior, and to see her strengths. These were, in fact, specific goals that had been set for all three group members.

Holliman's progress was demonstrated in his accounting of an outing with Tashi:

He announced that he had had a "very nice" time with Tashi, having taken her to the Scooper Bowl (a day when ice cream and cool drinks are available to children on the Boston Common) which they both enjoyed. It turned out to be a really fun day and they enjoyed one another, playing around together and "pigging out" on ice cream. Vivi and Thelma applauded Holliman's efforts, which pleased him.

Not long after, Holliman brought up his wish to arrange day camp for Tashi, taking the initiative to expose the child to positive, growth-producing experiences. Now he was no longer complaining about her, and did indeed seem to be understanding more about her needs and more about the many dimensions of parenting. He was far more accepting of parental responsibility, recognizing that he might be a single parent for a long time.

In a later session, he described a troubling decision he made to deny Tashi's mother a chance to be with her daughter:

Out of prison, she asked to come by for a visit. Reluctant and concerned, he nonetheless agreed, thinking that it was important for Tashi to see her mom. To his dismay, when her mother arrived, she wanted to take Tashi out for several hours and he noticed that a strange man was in the car. Feeling unsure that her mom was capable of protecting the child, Holliman refused to allow Tashi to leave home with her mom and this man. He described the disruption and the child's disappointment, but he had remained firm.

Vivi and Thelma immediately supported his good judgment as they considered with him the dangers this could have posed. Together they embraced Holliman as they congratulated him for his good judgment and for being protective of his daughter.

Coordinating the Process of the Parents' and Children's Groups

When parents brought up specific problem behaviors of the children in their group, the practitioner leading the children's group was alerted so that she could structure the group process to offer an opportunity for the child to learn more appropriate behaviors, thereby providing a concerted effort to help the family. Not only had Tashi's behavior problems become known to the practitioners of both groups, they also knew about Holliman's responses to these behaviors and structured the processes in both groups to focus on strategies that might help both father and child. For example, the parents' group practitioner informed her counterpart about the emphasis being placed on helping the father adopt more caring responses, giving warm, positive reinforcement to his daughter. In turn, the practitioner in the children's group placed emphasis on helping the daughter, Tashi, participate less aggressively with other children, using that group as a forum for setting limits positively and constructively. Both practitioners were thus focusing on improving family relationships and encouraging appropriate behavioral changes.

The two practitioners observed the progress of father and daughter through their reports to the group. For example, when Tashi received stars for improved behavior at school, she proudly placed the stars on her shoes so that they would "really stick" long enough for her to get them home to show off to her father and grandmother. Holliman, beaming with pride, brought this up in a group session, while the children's group also heard the story from Tashi.

The task of both practitioners was to compare clinical notes and to keep monitoring progress. They reviewed the home situation and the stressors stemming from the mother/grandmother's attitude about sharing her son, Holliman. There was agreement that the parents' group practitioner would push on employment and housing opportunities. (The grandmother was not considered a viable candidate for group service nor for other clinical work).

In fact, identifying resources, connecting clients to them, and advocating for clients were significant tasks of both practitioners.[2] The children's group practitioner was extremely active in arranging resources, getting E, Vivi's son, into intensive child therapy to address his deep-rooted psychological problems, arranging coverage through Medicare and also arranging for transportation. Both practitioners reinforced with Vivi the need for her son to be in therapy.

The parents' group was a support for Vivi who had initially not been able to reveal her young son's problems. Helping Holliman appeared to heighten her comfort and sense of trust. Thelma also had a sense of shame that David had secretly witnessed his father sexually abusing her. In time, she also opened up and let go of some of her anger, hurt, and disappointment. Holliman, eager to help them and reciprocate their support of him, conveyed to Thelma "how sorry I feel," while encouraging Vivi to continue pursuing help for E.

The literature on African-American males recognizes their reluctance to seek out help.[3] While earlier research has substantiated this fact, there is growing awareness that these men *will* participate when practitioners are skillful, culturally sensitive, and able to make appropriate use of their professional power.[4] Holliman, an intelligent, caring, single father, obviously overwhelmed and with no supports, struggling with parenting issues and unemployment, became able to connect with the two overwhelmed women. This is a different image than that characteristic of many inner-city males who must struggle to overcome effects of stereotypes. It is also different from the men involved with members of the Women Moving Forward group presented earlier who were unwilling to join a group and take advantage of the opportunity for growth.

Practitioners' Roles: Sobriety Group, Parent Education/Growth Group

In the sobriety group the practitioners assumed the role of facilitator, drawing on years of experience guided largely by psycho-dynamic and cognitive theories and knowledge of substance abuse. In contrast, the practitioners in the parent education/growth group also drew upon psycho-dynamic and cognitive theories. However in their work with overwhelmed clients they were required to have at their command extensive knowledge of concrete helping resources: financial aid such as AFDC, Medicare, Medicaid, and housing subsidies; community resources such as Head Start, employment options, day camp, and child care; educational resources including schools and training programs; and medical/health care resources such as HMOs and community clinics. These practitioners also demonstrated skill in negotiating these complex service delivery systems which required them to have knowledge of definitions or terms of eligibility, to build contacts and relationships with staff in large bureaucracies, and to be capable and willing to serve as advocates for their clients, helping them learn skills in navigating such systems.[5] In other words, these practitioners were committed to justice-based service.

Outcome

What was accomplished? In the sobriety group members made strides through group interaction on their problems with relationships, improving interpersonal competence, resolving lifelong conflicts and anger toward parents, and developing significant self-knowledge.

Of course the bottom line was to maintain sobriety and to receive support in this endeavor. The therapist-informant reports that over 90 percent were able to achieve sobriety. This constitutes a stronger outcome than for most groups, probably because most members remained in treatment for the initial three-month commitment and some stayed longer. Patients who are persuaded, encouraged, or even coerced into treatment by those important to them are more apt to remain in treatment and to have a better prognosis than those that are not so pressured.[6] The 90 percent also includes those who had a drinking slip but continued group treatment and achieved long-term sobriety before terminating.

True to its name, the Black-Hispanic Parent Education/Growth group was able to nurture its members, assisting them as overwhelmed single parents to expand their repertoire of child management skills and to see and have rewarding, enriching life experiences with their children.

What was so impressive in this group is that a male who had experienced negative relationships with his mother and his wife was able to receive support and encouragement from two women, one of whose cultural background differed from his own. Indeed we make the point that mixed-gender groups, carefully convened, have much to offer the single, overwhelmed, African-American male. We see also how such clients can grow and learn to parent effectively a young female child.

Few cases exist in the literature that examine these dynamics: far from the stereotype of the complacent abandoning father, this client was able to achieve a higher level of functioning as a result of a trusting group and sound intervention executed by a practitioner who believed in her client's strengths.

These two groups offer differing pictures of clinical processes. One was marked by sophisticated verbal exchange and dialogue in using the group to gain self-knowledge. In the other group clients explored issues stemming from problems experienced at a different level of the social system than those experienced by the sobriety group members. This latter group, the Black-Hispanic Parent Education/Growth group, was marked by mutuality and highly active support which was exhibited not only by the practitioner/leader but also by the members. It was also characterized by basic hands-on support, a different degree of personal sharing, and a different level of closeness.[7] The reputed differences in culture and class dynamics appear to be substantiated here.

7

THE GANG GROUPS

Examples and Strategies for Change
Through Group Intervention and
Community Building

While the focus of this book is the use of groups as a resource for therapeutic intervention and problem solving for people, we present in this chapter an examination of a type of group process that is a problem for society and at the same time serves as a short-term solution for certain overwhelmed youth: the gang. We also present a therapeutic group developed to rehabilitate gang members and note some efforts and partnerships for community building which we hope will thwart gang development.

WHY GANGS?

Indeed the gang is viewed by society as a troubling, growing menace. In this chapter we discuss the gang as a unique group that uses many wiles to entrap youth in its web. Antisocial though gangs are, practitioners need to understand the power and attraction of gangs in order to develop the therapeutic intervention and community-building strategies needed to combat the forces that create the gang groups. To many youths gangs offer a refuge from structural problems: weakened urban infrastructure, changing demographics, and ineffective service systems including schools, police, and public maintenance services for streets and parks. The lack of legitimate work opportunities means the underground economy represents more stature to a poor, troubled youth. The gang also provides needed connectedness and serves as a surrogate family for many.

For decades, gang researchers and theorists have helped create the impression, if not the stereotype, that gangs provide a haven for only overwhelmed, ghetto-based youths of color looking for opportunities to break out of poverty. Several theories attempt to explain why youths are attracted to gangs: Among these are flight from dysfunctional families and personal survival (dysfunctional family theory); access to work even if illegal—drug trading, car stealing, etc.—in the absence of legitimate economic options (strain theory); participation in a marginal environment that accepts/tolerates deviant behaviors (cultural deviance theory); and finally, the drive for affiliation, identification, validation, belonging, and purpose (psychological affiliation theory). Personal safety is another significant reason youth join gangs. There are, no doubt, other dimensions of gang attraction that we have not comprehended fully. One such aspect is the movement of gangs beyond inner-city ghettos and ethnic neighborhoods into the city at large where white youths are joining gangs. Suburban youth, African-American and white, are joining gangs known as "black gangs"; white youth from more affluent surroundings are perhaps joining up out of loss of community, the need for adventure, self-defense owing to gang expansion, opportunity to act on racial prejudices and fears, access to drug money, or all of these mentioned. There is no way of determining the extent to which and in what combinations geography, ethnicity, poverty, racism, security, and the quest for drugs and capital converge and propel individuals into ganging.[1] Certainly pop culture plays a role in painting gangs as attractive groups.

Other, more provocative questions might be raised about organizations whose members are white, polarized politically, and who espouse racial supremacy and hatred and are known to be dangerous, but who are not usually referred to as gangs. Skinheads and militia would be examples; perhaps the oldest gang would be the Ku Klux Klan (KKK).[2] A distinguishing feature of the latter, however, was that it traditionally acted as an unacknowledged extension of the established community rather than in defiance of it.

While we acknowledge these limitations in our discussion on gangs, this chapter will focus, nonetheless, on an urban gang and on the difficulties and opportunities that confront practitioners and society in reaching gang members and helping them to change and to embrace more socially acceptable behavior patterns.

Gang researcher Carl Taylor has developed a gang typology and outlined the attributes unique to each as follows: One is the *scavenger* gang which does not have goals, purpose, or even substantial camaraderie, and often engages in senseless, spontaneous crimes. Members usually struggle with homelessness, school failure, and personal problems. Within this type of gang little or no leadership and organizational structure are manifested. A second is the *territorial* gang which usually focuses on ownership of an area. Protection of members and maintenance and identification regarding that which is owned are forces that hold this type of gang together. A third is the *commercial* gang which traffics in drugs, for-hire murder, or other activities for material gain. Yet another gang is the *corporate* gang which also has financial gain through criminal actions as its reason for existence; however its infrastructure is not unlike that of a legal corporation. Camaraderie and socialization of members, while valuable characteristics, are not what drive this gang; financial gain, capitalism, and control of a market are the preeminent forces. An example is the Mafia.[3]

Below we discuss in some detail the organizational structure, leadership, and other dynamics of a gang in the Boston area. The material gathered indicates that this gang corresponds most closely, but not exclusively, to the territorial gang which protects its turf largely for the sale of drugs. This gang also provides a protective function, serving as surrogate family to many youth whose own families remain seriously overwhelmed.

THE S STREET LIONS FAMILY: GANG RECRUITMENT, STRUCTURE, ORGANIZATION, AND PROTECTIVE FUNCTION

A practitioner who worked with troubled youth stated, "It's sad—the gang is the only family these kids know. There is no parent to teach them morals and decent behavior. What they know is from the streets."

The structure of many Boston gangs is seen by practitioners as less formal than many across the nation (for example, West Coast gangs). The hierarchy is similar to organizations such as the Masons and Elks fraternal organizations that are popular in many communities—these gangs have a king and a treasurer. Several Boston gang groups tend to be territorial, often taking the name of the street on which members reside. Another name may then be added—perhaps an animal such as "panther" or "bear" or "lion."[4] Today there may be no easily discernible dress that allows law enforcement to identify members. Mainstreaming fashion by many youth has made gang dress codes less significant.[5]

A major force shaping the gang group is its community context. Gangs may now include children as young as five or six to up to age 25 and older—unlike earlier gangs where members outgrew the organization as they matured from adolescence into adulthood. All know how the gang operates from early information shared by siblings, cousins, or neighbors. They know the risks: beatings, wars, and even death. They know the benefits: drugs, money, friendship, nice cars, and expensive gold jewelry. They know too that they can get it all quickly, attaining high status without much productive work, although there is considerable risk.

Though money is available through gang activity, it is hardly sufficient to propel most members and their families out of poverty and their marginal economic status. The funds circulating and flowing through the Boston gang discussed here in no way compare with the $100 million supposedly controlled by the Chicago-based Gangster Disciples, and only small sums trickle down to the average member. Gang members hang out together, from doorsteps to the street corner, starting at preschool. They grow up with one another, living in the care of each other, and eventually become supportive if not devoted to one another. Though socialized in the gang culture, members nonetheless go through initiation rites, some of which, such as robbery and mugging, can be physically painful as well as harmful to others. Explaining the appeal of the gang, a youth worker commented on the way in which caring for younger children is a common practice: "The gang members do all the baby-sitting." He then elaborated:

Many gang members are treated harshly in their homes by their families. The gang is often more gentle, providing care that even includes food.

When such basic care is provided by the gang, no one should be surprised by the loyalty and commitment it engenders. Loyalty is evident and indeed demanded throughout the neighborhood, in schools, and in other locations where members move about, such as the beach or shopping malls. Access to public or private transportation has had a transforming impact on gangs, allowing members to move beyond their own neighborhood.[6]

On long streets and in areas where there are large numbers of children and youth, gang members "cover" certain corners or intersections. On one street in a certain section of the city there are five gangs, all making up what is known as the S Street Lions, somewhat like clans who come together as a tribe. It is these gangs who have served as a data source for this exploration. A major reason for such structure in gangs like the S Street Lions is the need to get around a law that identifies more than three as an illegal gathering.[7] While this law impacts the structure, organization, and movement of the gangs, the members' use of such small numbers as the cells of the gang group outfoxes both the law and law enforcement. With the members, there is a range of ages, interest, and involvement, with younger members often less involved than older ones.

Violence is apt to erupt when one gang moves onto another street in order to expand drug activity. Explained a youth worker: "Turf wars are very violent because all they [the gang members] have is their street [territory]." As their major possession, the "street" must be protected and defended by any means. "Any means" includes shooting people or destroying property if that is what is necessary to fend off rival gangs or persons who are suspected of having connections to police and other law enforcement agencies and personnel. Intergroup fights and conflict over particular turf arise out of the desire for control over territory and, in this instance, control of a greater share of the drug market.

Because most members of the five gangs making up the S Street

Lions are of school age, there is considerable impact on the schools and school grounds. These are considered part of the gang territory and thus are negatively affected. Much rivalry begins in the neighborhoods and is carried over into the schools—even in the elementary and the middle schools—creating significant barriers in the educational environment.

In this gang, members are idle much of the time, merely hanging out; when there is activity it is often drug related. At times interaction between gangs becomes violent for reasons other than "turfdom" and drugs—for example, when a member feels disrespected or "dissed" by a member of another gang. Usually, however, fights are about drugs, or settling old "beefs" that involved drugs. Given the extreme age range of members and the fairly loose structure of members' gatherings, two or three at a time, it is seldom that all members are involved in the same violent encounter. Although usually only one or two individuals may be involved, the violence can be deadly. But the development of the gang may not be as simple as it seems, owing to many complexities particularly around the issue of membership and different levels of interest, investment, and involvement. See Table 7–1.

Consider that many youths join a gang because they have few, if any, viable alternatives for securing nurturence and safety. Some may in fact maintain some psychological distance from the gang, resenting the intrusion that is embodied in belonging while at the same time being dependent upon the gang's resources. Such youngsters believe that they have no choice but to avow allegiance to the gang but there may be little commitment to its goals. They are entrapped. One practitioner with expertise in working with gang members stated:

> A kid will tell you he is in the gang when his friends are around. He can't lose face with his gangster friends. When alone, he may say he really isn't a real member—just hangs around. This type of kid is often helpful if you get a chance to speak with him alone.

This gang worker described this type of interchange between practitioner and gang member as a beginning point for exposing youths to ideas and options available through alternative programs. Such an encounter provides an opening to the professional helping relation-

TABLE 7–1

Levels of Gang Involvement

Level I: Fantasy Identification with Gang

1. Knows about gangs primarily from newspapers, newscasts, and the movies.
2. May know about "real" gangs.
3. May know gang members but does not associate.
4. May like, respect, or admire a gang, a gang member, or the gang lifestyle.
5. Sees gang members "living out a fantasy."

Level II: At Risk of Gang Involvement

1. Has personal knowledge of gangs and gang members.
2. Casually and occasionally associates with gang members.
3. Lives in or near gang areas (turfs).
4. May like or admire gangs or gang members as individuals.
5. May like or admire the gang's lifestyle but not fully participate.

Level III: Wanna-Be/Associate Gang Member

1. Personally knows and admires gang members.
2. Regularly associates with gang members.

cont'd

---

ship and at the same time it offers a beginning opportunity to learn about the youth's family situation.

> Sometimes a youth will let down and tell you how his friends take care of him. Other youths may try to be macho or real cool and tough, but underneath they are real scared. They are afraid of the gang's force and power and the actions the gang can take. At the same time they are afraid of the isolation from a parent or blood relatives.

In cases of such deep personal, psychological, and emotional conflict, it takes concerted discussion to help move this type of youth to alternative options. A major hindrance is that the youth has to come back to the streets, face his gang friends, and at the same time return to a home that may be nonsupportive. Facing this scenario, chances are he will go for the gang for safety, security, food, and escape from a

3. Considers gangs and related activity as normal, acceptable, or admirable.

4. Finds many things in common with gang members.

5. Is mentally prepared to join a gang.

Level IV: Gang Member

1. Is officially a gang member.

2. Associates almost exclusively with gang members to the exclusion of family and former friends.

3. Participates in gang crimes and other related activities.

4. Has substantially rejected the authority or value system of family and society.

5. Is not yet considered hard core by fellow gang members or others.

Level V: Hard-Core Gang Member

1. Is totally committed to the gang and gang lifestyle.

2. Totally rejects anyone or any value system other than the gang.

3. Is considered hard core by self, other gang members, and authorities.

4. Will commit any act with the approval or a demand from the gang.

5. Does not accept any authority other than the gang.

6. Has fully submerged personal goals for the collective goals of the gang.

Source: Boys and Girls Club of America, 1993. Reprinted by permission. From C. Branch (1997), "Clinical Interventions with Gang Adolescents and Their Families." Boulder, Colorado: Westview Press.

bad family life. For him, the gang may not be great or even the preferred option, but rather the only option. It is a sure thing. The gang is family, a guard against the chaotic community and other consequences of poverty and societal neglect.

The protective function that gangs serve is essential in the lives of the members and often misunderstood by outsiders. Not only is the community often chaotic—and the families within it too frequently underorganized,[8] poorly functioning, and overwhelmed—it is also dangerous. In this context the gang offers refuge and safety by functioning as it does as a shield from noxious, threatening influences—although initiation rites and other activities are often just as dangerous. One such influence that gang members fear is rival gangs, who out of necessity compete for turf, new members, and control of geographical areas including schools and school grounds, parks, streets, and alleys. Today, tools of control involve guns and knives and, in some areas of the city, vicious dogs such as pit bulls, Rottweilers, and Dobermans that have been bred and trained to fight.

We must underscore that while the gang is not as attractive to every member, getting out of it is often viewed as impossible. One member reported: "There is no way out of the gang—only by death. And, while in, you must do whatever is requested, or die." The gang represented absolute control to this member.

Goals: The Gang Agenda

In addition to serving as controller, protector, and nurturer, gangs generally have more specialized purposes. All members of the S Street Lions know that its goals are to maintain and expand turf, to sell drugs for profit, and to maintain a viable, strong membership in order to accomplish goals. The S Street Lions prefer to deal in crack cocaine, given its availability, competitive price, and reputation for delivering a quick high. Certain organizational structure and leader styles exist to enhance the gang's chances of success. Hanging out together all the time in small numbers is part of the structure, promoting continuous talk, enabling members to engage in spur of the moment drug sales, and preserving the capacity for reaction if a rival gang enters claimed turf. The S Street Lions adapt their structure to the law by restricting association on the streets to small numbers. Thus, they can move rapidly and without the awkwardness and suspicion inspired by larger numbers.

Leadership, Power and Control

The leader is the most respected member if not the smartest, physically strongest, or most violent. He gets his position based on his ability to solve problems. He could be the most violent of the members or the most knowledgeable about street life—of drug dealers and customers, and skills in ducking police or outplotting rival gangs. Particularly savvy about police, the leader possesses excellent intelligence regarding police interference and is probably also the most feared, capable of intimidating younger and weaker members and others. As noted above, given the need for control he is usually smart enough to bypass the temptations of drugs and alcohol, recognizing the need to be quick thinking and with a clear head. In some city gangs, midlevel lieutenants are required to stay away from drugs because using them can cause these members to face expulsion by the top leadership. To leaders, drugs are a personal liability. More attractive to them are power, money, and the materialistic rewards they bring. A fine car is highly prized. High-priced cars, always an attraction for teenage youth and young adults, generate more respect from the other members, other gangs, and girls. There is some indication that membership in the S Street Lions offered opportunity for greater access to sexual partners. The ultimate reward for leaders is influence over others, that is, power.

In the absence of constructive activities, some gang members hang out all the time, into the very early morning hours, and return again before day break. Much time is spent just hanging out in idle discussion. Sometimes discussion is sorting out drug or police tips. Many leaders are very successful in generating and sustaining profitable gang activity, and in avoiding gang workers and police filtration. Drug dealing is often spur of the moment activity, requiring ability to mobilize for fast action. Someone has to be "in charge" to call the shots and make deals. The leader and members review goals frequently, relative to drugs and turf, and scheme regarding how to move swiftly in order to conquer more territory.

In this gang, the leader's power is extreme and autocratic. The top leader, the king, has several lower-ranking functionaries, who regard him as the monarch. Having earned his position, because of entrepreneurial skills (negotiating good deals from drug suppliers and gun dealers), street cleverness (delivering a major increase in sale of drugs), or violence (beating, stabbing, or shooting competitors within the gang as well as with rival gangs), the king rules with awesome control. As leader he calls the shots in order to accomplish the gang's mission. Leaders find it essential to maintain strong internal control.

The hierarchical organization is fundamental to the operation of the S Street Lions, helping to keep the membership in line. The vertical structure for distribution of drugs allows leaders to maintain control because there is competition among the lower echelons. Some members are always willing to do more work and expand drug sales. And there are always people at the lower levels hoping to earn a greater volume of drug sales, obtaining more and higher status. Rational though they are and clever too, members do get apprehended by police, at which time they become vulnerable to the power of a different organized force. Some are able to withstand interrogation and maintain secrecy. Others are not. The gang leader uses such situations to demonstrate additional political skills, helping secure bail money for the jailed member, helping families make contact with attorneys who want this business. The leader uses such situations also to set up communication—passing along information to those in jail. Skills at connecting members and reducing isolation are important to members who face a controlled environment.

It is at such times that the leader, with the assistance of the treasurer, demonstrates resourcefulness and reliability. These activities assume the capacity for securing money when needed. Good attorneys are expensive and bail is apt to be high, especially when neighborhood organizations and the press are making noise. At such times, the law enforcement and judicial systems are apt to hand out higher bail and heavier sentences. When funds are low because of slack drug sales and competition from rival gangs, members are forced into other activities (car theft, robbery, and mugging) or the top leaders may be able to negotiate loans with local drug suppliers and gun dealers.

The decline of legitimate work and the growth of drug markets have made the sale of drugs important gang work. Members are expected to turn their receipts over to the king and the treasurer. Both are responsible for dispersing funds in ways that meet the needs of the gang (i.e., a little extra money to members whose family are more needy or experiencing a crisis, and portions for individual gang members). The competition related to moving up and gaining power is tremendous. When members fail to turn sales money over, serious internal conflict is engendered. Members who are accused of stealing, cheating, cutting corners, and running games are dealt with severely by the leaders. In the S Street Lions, additional internal "beefs" often arose out of competition over girls, and from violation of gang codes such as giving hints or tips to rival gang members or police infiltrators. The latter constitutes a far more serious infraction.

"Beefs"

For many gangs internal "beefs" can be handled in a number of ways, with responses that are usually more situational than ritualistic, including withdrawal of rewards, especially friendship, safety, and money which deprives a member of essentials. Extreme methods of internal conflict management, such as the burning of body parts, are not uncommon. For example, one gang member of the S Street Lions, Sam, had committed an infraction and knew he had to face punishment. Realizing that he would be corrected by the gang, he decided to withdraw from gang activities. He stopped hanging out, remaining at first within the confines of his building and then only in his apartment, small and crowded though it was. Later Sam moved in with relatives on another street in the same geographical area. In spite of his caution, the gang found him and administered third degree burns to one hand as his "just" punishment during a ritual witnessed by his old gang group. This ritual was to "teach" him, and just as importantly to "warn" others of the gang leader's control and the gang's power and capacity for personal violence. It was reported that the status of this particular wayward gang member was such that he constituted a threat to members because he knew secrets that would be of interest to police or a rival gang. These secrets would most likely involve information about drugs—sellers, buyers, big suppliers—important and secret information. Although he had been a threat, his position had not been high enough to warrant that he be immediately gunned down. Nonetheless, such a fate might still be his one day, an illustration of the way in which violence escalates as situations become more and more complex. In this instance the motivation for the hand burning was punishment and the response of the former member with the burned hand will probably be revenge. What form his retaliation will take is not clear. Could he become a police informer? Might he retaliate alone? Or might he help out another gang? Indeed, the tendency to engage in retaliatory behavior is not unlike the behavior that is condoned in some fundamentalist faiths—cutting off the hand for stealing, or an "eye for an eye."

Guns

A major issue in the activity of gangs is the use of guns. A 13-year-old states: "I saw my cousin get shot." A 14-year-old states: "I saw my cousin get shot."

Used to help members hold on to their turf, guns are big among the S Street Lions and as one practitioner with expertise in gangs has suggested: "Guns are the enforcers." In the past, gang members used their fists, boards, bats, or knives to settle "beefs." Now guns are the weapon of choice. Many gangs have automatic firearms that fire multiple rounds and can be reloaded quickly. The practitioner emphasized: "The bigger the gun, the better." Through "beefing," a gang member can settle up with words, tough and nasty though they may be. However if that member has a weapon, he can probably cause the other to retreat, but this might escalate if the latter comes back later with a weapon. The spiral grows, with violence breeding violence.

A Note About Female Associates

Females are also part of the scene and dynamics of the gang. Gun selling is embraced in order to maintain turf and/or control a drug market, and girls are heavily involved as accessories, holding weapons, or buying and selling them. The females associated with the S Street Lions had not organized their own gang structure and organization (a phenomenon that is growing) but were instead auxiliaries and important auxiliaries (neither were they members in the sense of a mixed gender or coed gang).[9] Thus, in addition to the gun activity, they constituted important communication links passing information and messages to gangsters, a particularly sensitive assignment whenever normal tensions among rival gangs become exacerbated. They also assume dangerous roles for themselves and their sex partners, especially during initiation rites of males, and they may be involved in offenses against property, but they are not generally killers.[10] Experts suggest that in some cases, girls are used as chattel.[11] In this context, a concern of those providing service to gang members and their girlfriends is the frequency of risky, even deadly, sexual activity. A new member might start having unprotected sex, even group sex, to comply with the initiation ritual.

Women and girls were mostly viewed and treated as property or chattel as noted earlier. This is not to suggest that females are passive. Affiliation with gang members offers protection and money, and these women are assertive. To get money they assume active roles, even suggesting drug-related actions. They may fight among themselves over the guys since status is associated with whom one goes out with. The bottom line, though, is that they are unequal partners. What puzzled us was why these women had not organized as an independent gang given the current societal emphasis on women's rights and their experience in families that may have been as dysfunctional as those of the male gangsters. Our assumption is that they derived sufficient satisfaction from their minimum economic and social roles as auxiliaries.

Some women suffer losses through death of a lover, brother, other relative, or friend. Those who have borne children face a difficult future, which the gang helps with by serving as family and by sporadically providing limited funds. But such a loss leaves a child fatherless while the woman is left to form another alliance. The disruption, disorganization, and heavy burdens continue.

Females joined males in risky and dangerous sexual behavior, allowing themselves to be used for sex in exchange for money, drugs, and nice material goods. It does not register with some of these women that none of the rewards is worth the price of flirting with HIV/AIDS. Social agencies may be missing an important service opportunity by not targeting specific social services, health and education programs to this population of needful girls and women.

STRATEGIES FOR INTERVENTION:
CHANGING THE GANG CULTURE

Given the structure of the S Street Lions, it is understandable how difficult it is for practitioners and those engaged in preventive work such as ministers, the police, etc., to infiltrate gangs: drugs and guns make gang work infinitely harder and more unsafe than in the past. The ambiance they create is vastly more dangerous than that found in the gang culture of earlier days, making much of what was known about gangs obsolete today. However, some interventions hold promise as noted below.

Two types of strategies for changing the gang culture merit exploration: One, used in the Boston area, is President Clinton's model for a national campaign against youth crime; the other is in Syracuse, New York. The former focuses more on the community and law enforcement; the latter on clinical intervention with gang members. We discuss the clinical intervention first.

THE THERAPEUTIC GROUP[12]

Goals

The main goal of the therapeutic group is to supply a sense of community for violence-prone youth and to meet the human needs that gang membership has provided and that have been otherwise missing in their lives. Objectives are realistic. The first is longevity of life and survival and the second is that members live to teach other (new and potential) members how to get what they need in socially sanctioned forms. Several practitioners with gang youth note that with death so prevalent in overwhelmed communities, many youth do not expect long life and some do not think of life beyond ages 20 to 25. It is not unusual for youth to think and behave as if they are terminally ill. Related to the second objective is the goal of identifying and then focusing on what is good in their experience and applying it to other parts of their lives and daily activities.

Referrals, Screening, and Assessment

The juvenile justice system and public schools refer youth to this program, including those who have been incarcerated. The initial screening evaluates potential for suicide and the significance of a history of uncontrollable temperament. If these conditions are identified, youths are directed to individual treatment prior to assignment in the group.

The purpose of therapy is carefully explained using language that appeals to youth, such as this metaphor about help for an ailing body part: "One must prepare for surgery; likewise, one must prepare for the group." Also evaluated in the screening/assessment is the youths' developmental stage of relationship capacity. Youths who appear highly narcissistic and who only think of themselves are referred for individual therapy, since extreme self-orientation can mean danger to others, the community, and themselves.

As the group starts, contact is made with the family to prepare members for the point in time when the youth has completed therapy, is ready to terminate from the group, and has also given up the gang. Thus, another goal is to expand the intervention from work with the group to work with the family. If the biological family is unwilling or unable to reaccept the youth, alternative families such as extended family, uncles, aunts, or church members are sought. The practitioner makes the push to locate a good family, believing that there is always someone out in the community who can help.

Membership Composition

The group is open-ended with a membership of eight to ten participants. A few members continue in the group for as long as a year. Usually, those youths who are more disconnected from their families remain in the group the longest time. Youths can be usually identified as Level IV or V, as noted in Table 7–1.

The Model

In this innovative therapeutic group with gang members, colleagues at Syracuse University have offered a model for the conceptualization of violence which is applicable to gang-prone or gang-active youth. Hardy and Laszloffy[13] argue that four aggravating factors, when they are combined and interact, increase the likelihood of violence among troubled adolescents: devaluation, disruption or erosion of community, unmourned loss, and rage.

Devaluation occurs when the worth and integrity of a person or group is assaulted and denigrated. Adolescents who have painful experience with being devalued as individuals, and/or by virtue of their membership in various groups (e.g., racial, gender, economic) are at increased risk of violence.

. . . Community is the place where individuals derive their sense of connectedness and belonging. Hardy and Laszloffy (In Press) have identified three different levels of community, primary (e.g., familial), extended (e.g., neighborhoods, schools), and cultural (e.g., racial, gender, economic), which provide adolescents with a sense of identity and connection to the world around them. When disruption or erosion occurs in one or all of these levels, it increases the risk of adolescent violence.

Unacknowledged, unmourned, and unhealed loss of any kind also increases the risk of adolescent violence. Losses can be physical, as in the case of the death of a loved one, or emotional/psychological, as in the loss of dignity or respect. Adolescents who have losses that remain unacknowledged, unmourned, and unhealed, also are at a risk of violence. Experiences with loss inevitably produce feelings of pain, grief, and rage. When loss remains unacknowledged and unhealed, these feelings tend to be denied, suppressed, or minimized. Unfortunately, when rage in particular is denied expression, it intensifies. Hence, when loss remains unacknowledged and unhealed, feelings of rage tend to build until they eventually explode, often resulting in violence.

The practitioners who developed this model have labeled it "VCR" for the stages of intervention which include validation, confrontation, and restoration in the community.

Group Process

From early work with the model the practitioners learned that it is essential to offer support and help that confirm one's sense of self before confronting, and challenging youth. This is the validation stage of the model.

Early Stage

In the early part of the process group members develop, with the help of the leader, a loss diagram which is a picture that shows the people whom each youth has lost. Similar to a genogram (diagram of relationships within a given family), the loss diagram begins with the individual instead of with earlier generations. Instead of the vertical structure

FIGURE 7–1

Loss Diagram from Hardy and Laszloffy

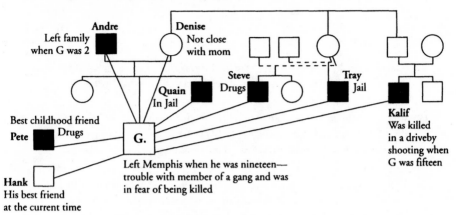

of a genogram the horizontal structure shows the losses that have occurred around them, starting with their peers and eventually moving to
a focus on their families. Because they are encouraged to deal with their
feelings of loss first about peers and others not so close and then the
family, the issue of mourning and feeling the painful associated feelings
is less frightening. Youth are then able to mourn the loss of persons
who were close more adequately. Figure 7–1 is an example of the Loss
Diagram; Table 7–2 shows how the practitioners help youths move
through this therapeutic exercise.

The primary intent of the validation stage is to facilitate management of rage and loss. Attention is not given to violence; the practitioner gets at violence by an initial focus on rage and loss. There is no
challenge or criticism until each youth feels validated concerning his
painful experience. Hardy suggests:

> A thread of criticism weighs heavily on a devalued person. Thus, the group
> leader must absorb their disrespect.

The practitioner's goal is to find something about the youth to au-
thentically validate him. The effort is to find and identify a strength.
For example:

TABLE 7–2

Loss Diagram

Kenneth V. Hardy. Ph.D.** Tracey A. Laszloffy, M.A.**

Violence is fortified when a person is anesthetized to her/his loss.

Goal: To assess the level of loss in a client's life; to ascertain if mourning was able to occur, and if so, how?; to begin the process of helping the client to feel her/his loss and engage in mourning it adequately.

Construct a genogram-like diagram of the client and the significant people in his/her life. Identify where losses occurred in person's life. Use different colors to distinguish between different types of loss. For instance, use one color for physical loss and another for emotional loss.

a) This is similar to a genogram except that rather than beginning with earlier generations, it begins with the client. In this sense it is focused on the "here and now"—it looks at their life horizontally as opposed to the traditional vertical orientation of a genogram.

b) To begin assessing the level of loss start by focusing on peers instead of family because this is potentially less threatening.

Suggested Questions for Conducting a Loss Diagram:

Who were your friends in first grade? Who was your best friend?

How many of your friends from first grade do you still have today? Where are they now, what are they doing?

How many friends from first grade did you lose contact with? Do you have any knowledge of why you lost contact with one another? Do you know what became of them?

What did you and (name of best friend) do for fun back in those days? [trying to assess what was important to the person to get clues about what might have been lost]

When you were in first grade, where did you live and where did you go to school?

Back in first grade when (name of friend) was your best friend, how did you get to school? [making shift from peers to family]

How did (name of friend) get to school?

Back when __ was your best friend, what family members do you remember the most? [making shift from peers to family]

What family members were you closest to when you were in the first grade?

What was it like at home when you were in the first grade? How did everyone get along with each other? What were your relationships like with each of those family members?

Do you still live in the same house you lived in when you were in first grade?

Do you still live in the same neighborhood you lived in when you were in first grade? [making shift from family to community]

How often do you still pass by the school you went to in first grade?

So now you are __ years old. [making shift from past to present]

How many of your friends from first grade do you still have today? __ Are you still friends with (name of best friend?

Of the friends that you lost contact with, do you know why this happened?

How many friends did you have who have died? __ How did they die?

How many friends have you lost due to drugs? __; moving away __; some other reasons __?

And today, tell me about your relationships with each family member now?

How many family members do you know who died in your lifetime? __ How did they die?

How many family members have you lost due to drugs? __; divorce/separation __; moving away? __; doesn't/don't get along with you? __

As you reflect upon this exercise and the diagram we have constructed, what does it say to you about your experiences with loss? What thoughts and feelings have been stimulated for you?

Which of these losses have you had opportunities to grieve or mourn? How did you do that and what effect did this have? And which losses have remained unacknowledged/unmourned, and what effect has that had?

Who was home after school was over?

So now you are __ years old. Where is (name of friend) now?

What about other friends that you have or had, where are they?

Back when __ was your best friend, what family members do you remember the most?

And today, what are your thoughts/feelings about those family members?

Tell me about your relationship with each of your family members.

How many people (friends or otherwise) do you know who have been killed or have died? __; committed suicide? __; on drugs? __; moved away? __

How many family members do you know who have been killed or have died in your lifetime? __; committed suicide? __; on drugs? __; moved away? __; you or a member of your family don't/doesn't get along with? __

**Slocum Hall, Syracuse University, Syracuse, New York 13244; Phone: 315-443-3023 Fax: 315-443-2562

A youth might stand with his back to you saying "F— you!" But, that youth has been able to come to talk with me and he is in the room with me. This is a positive step, and is built upon.

A major strength to be built upon is loyalty. Another example of validation involves work that was done with the family of a client using a gang member in the role of helper, as described by Hardy.

> I met with a family of a self-referred mother who asked me to help her get her son out of a gang. I was accompanied to the family session by a gang member whom I had recruited. The gang youth talked in the session about the usefulness of gangs and what was good about them. A major theme was loyalty. What was critical here was that the mother heard that what her child was looking for was unconditional commitment.

Once a child feels validated, meaning that some of his strengths are recognized and that he feels respected, the focus can move to confrontation.

Middle Stage

Confrontation is the time of actual challenge to youth about dangers, risks, and the actual costs related to certain thoughts and—more critically—actions. Confrontation addresses the actual gang activity. Using the strengths that have been recognized, youth are then asked "to look at the other side." For example they might be told:

> The loyalty to the gang is commendable and useful because you have someone to watch your back. But, can you be the individual you would like to be in the gang? Can you go play basketball with friends when you want? Can you take your little brother out?

Once youths begin to entertain the possibility that the gang may not be best for them, a critical point has been reached. Now, the family must be approached to reintegrate the youth. Work with the families is designed to help them appreciate the changes that youths have made, and also to change the manner in which family members interact with the youth that may have promoted the flight to the gang. What this means is that the family very often has to change as much as the youth. Still, during this middle stage where the focus is *confrontation* moving toward *restoration,* the process is fragile indeed, and the outcome is still in doubt. The issue is this: can the family commit to the youth and can the youth give up the gang? Thus, the intervention continues with the group to facilitate conditions that will make it more attractive for the youth to give up the gang. The extensive work with the families facilitates a smoother transition from the gang, a pseudo-community, to a real community. When there are signs of a clear commitment to the family, and vice versa, a youth is prepared to leave the group. However, since connections are important, the youth is encouraged to stay in touch. For example, the youth may be asked to come back to the agency since he is now in a position to help others and give something back:

> *In one case, **H.**, a youth who had successfully given up the gangs, was asked to come back to the agency and help to recruit a youngster to group treatment who was in danger of engaging in violence. The problem was with a 13-year-old who viewed his gang as a "posse," and was committed to revenge. H. was told: "We can't reach this 13-year-old, we think that you can." H. agreed to try. He wrote the 13-year-old a letter in which, sounding very much like a father or older brother, he noted that he had been a prisoner and was interested in helping him, encouraging the 13-year-old to come to the group. This interaction worked.*

Rules and Clear Communication

In this therapeutic group, strong support was offered but there were also high expectations about group members' capacities and strengths. One very important rule related to weapons. The practitioner advised emphatically that guns should not be brought to the group. He explains to the group: "I'm scared of guns. I cannot think when I'm scared. I have the same reaction to guns as I do when I have to go to the bathroom."

This practitioner was specific and direct. Throughout the group process, he used language that the youth understood. Ridding oneself of anger was expressed as "removing stingers"; bumbles referred to "bumble bees." It was important for members and practitioner to communicate and there was no place for misunderstanding.

Final Stage and Outcome

It becomes particularly difficult to achieve a successful outcome when the families of these youth cannot sufficiently reconnect with them. It is also difficult when, despite a reconnection, a youth finds it hard to give up the gang affiliation and rewards, including money from drug sales and other perks, at the same time that there are no jobs: the likelihood of a positive outcome is seriously jeopardized. These circular, entrapping forces often militate against success with group intervention.

Hardy has observed that in the use of this intervention, six out of ten will have successful outcomes, i.e., they will give up their gang activity. The other four have such massive disconnection or will be unable to extricate themselves from gang activity so that, unfortunately, they will move deeper into personal and community violence.

THE CENTRALITY OF FAMILY IN WORK WITH GANG YOUTH

Practitioners must obviously examine a youth's circumstances, paying attention not just to the individual behaviors both in and out of the gang but to the various systems that impact the lives of gang youth. These include family, neighborhood, and larger community systems; both personal/familial and societal/structural deficits must become units of attention.

The practitioner implementing the validation-confrontation-restoration model placed emphasis on involving the family in work with gang youth. Similarly, the worker making contact with the S Street Lions tried to assess a gang member's family life, often receiving data that suggested serious dysfunction in the family's way of functioning.

A number of questions that practitioners might explore in working with gang youth and their families in the effort to understand how both think of themselves have been suggested by Branch as follows:

Preintervention

The clinician needs to gain a clear understanding of how the family perceives itself. Those perceptions often become the basis of family interactions with outside entities, such as schools, courts, and mental health professionals. Following is a list of questions the clinician may want to consider asking before and after working with a family. Answers to the questions can be obtained from direct verbal reports as well as from observations of the family.

1. What is the structural hierarchy in the family? (Who makes the major decisions in the family? When does the power shift? Are family members aware of the power structure?)

2. Does everyone accept his or her role in the family?

3. How much influence do exosystems (i.e., parents' places of employment, adolescents' peer groups, the gang) have on the family's cohesiveness?

4. How does the family see itself as a unit?

5. How does the family think it is regarded by neighbors? What is its response to neighbors?

Postintervention

One of the anticipated outcomes of a family intervention is that the unit will develop new ways of being with itself and others. It is to be hoped that at the conclusion of clinical work with a family some new insights and behavioral changes will occur. To determine if there had been growth in the family, the clinician may want to repeat the preintervention assessment questions *plus* ask the following:

1. What significant behavioral changes have occurred in the family during the course of the clinical work? How does the family explain those changes? Feel about those changes?

2. Is there a change in the level of introspection in family members or increased perspective taking?[14] (Branch p131)

In using this tool, practitioners should be mindful of Aponte's message which concerns disruption and lack of organization in many families.[15] They should also note that overwhelmed families live with multiple environment stressors that sap their strengths, creating long-term, insidious, and progressively adverse consequences for their offspring. Interventions must be directed to healing and restoring the family, focusing on developing cohesion and the absence of discord, and developing communities that can protect families in ways that will support harmonious, nurturing relationships.

Boston Initiatives

Strategies to combat the rapidly escalating phenomenon of gangs and which are designed to offer gang groups an alternative for law-abiding, violence-free lives are spreading nationwide. The Crime Bill of 1994 endorsed community patrolling which has meant that many big city police departments are now struggling to bring back the beat cop, who functioned as a protector and, though transient, was known to residents.[16] The community policing initiative is based on a partnership among law enforcement agencies, schools, social agencies, and community groups.

The two initial members of the partnership were the police and probation departments and their major activity was making sure that youth adhered carefully to terms of probation or parole. This involved home visits in the evening to determine that youth were present and off the street. Gradually, this level of monitoring led to more discussion between the officers and youth. Becoming increasingly aware of gang members' home life, law enforcement agencies began reaching out to the community where organizations had already mobilized in an effort to address the gang situation.

This initiative highlights the need for a concerted attack: prevention, intervention to help youths in trouble, and effective, tough enforcement when youths have not been responsive to these first two strategies. Professionals are trained to respect each other and work cooperatively and in partnership, sharing responsibilities along with using approaches that involve working with community leaders and connecting with youths. As a result, officers in the Youth Violence Task Force have been acknowledged by residents for their assistance to youth. These officers have been recognized and rewarded for their efforts in steering vulnerable youths in helpful, constructive directions (away from gangs and into alternative activities) and in learning about the difficult home and neighborhood forces that entrap them and contribute to the attraction of a gang. Alternative activities for gang youth include such programs as Peace League Basketball, which teaches a conflict resolution curriculum, and the Summer of Opportunity Program where a partnership involving police, an insurance company, an urban university, and corporations offer life skills training and gainful employment to forty gang members. Prevention initiatives also include programs where youth service officers engage in conflict resolution approaches and enrichment activities with youths through bowling and basketball leagues, gang resistance work in schools, and placement in summer camps, all of which are viewed as paying positive dividends. Similar programs are available to help youths who are already in difficulty with gangs by offering diversion alternatives. Youths who are not willing to change gangster and criminal behaviors despite the offer of these options can face harsh consequences if apprehended, such as being jailed for long periods of time.[17]

One gang worker who works in a program for incarcerated youths, observed that:

> Many community residents and parents feel that sending youth away for long periods is unfair and unjust; I think of this program as a way to keep gangster, violence-oriented youths alive. For some, detention provides the first environment where youths know they will get a full meal, hot shower, and have some safe space. Not great, but better than they had.
>
> Some of the youth will tell you when they start talking to you that they don't want to get knocked off by some gang member. But, there ought to be services for poor youths. Rich kids get help. Their folks can buy it. A year round camp with strong academics, an exercise program, and job training would be ideal. A number of tough, financially well off kids get sent away to such programs by their families. These inner city youth really need a chance. They were born into bad circumstances.

One youth worker reported using the following approach to conflict resolution training. When youths were assembled, some looking unenthusiastic and even bored, he would have them stand.

He would tell them, "When you find yourself in a conflictual situation, look down, quickly, at your feet. You are all wearing sneakers that cost you $150.00. Use them—jet out!

"It is better to stay away from conflict. It can and will save your life."

The *first step* is to help youth expand friendships and learn something about trust (building trust) which is sorely lacking among these young people.

A trust exercise is conducted. Youths are paired off back to back in a double circle. One youth is told to fall and his partner catches him. Partners exchange positions and move on to other partners. Youth learn that they can depend on others and trust one another to respond to them when in need. As the trust exercise is repeated, some camaraderie finally develops and barriers are broken down. This takes time—hours and hours, weeks and weeks.

A few youth resist participating in the trust exercise, and they are helped in smaller sessions.

A *second step* is to help youth engage in discourse about violence. Why carry knives? Guns? That much maligned term, low self-esteem, surfaces as rationale for these behaviors.

Yet a *third step* is to help youth begin to think about positive alternatives. They are asked to dialogue about school, job-training, and work. The focus is on a positive future.

It was reported that before the advent of community-oriented programs law enforcement personnel sometimes intervened by picking up gang youths on minor traffic violations and getting them sent away as a way of offering protection. Such a solution was used in instances where the officer determined that the youngster was at particular risk for harming others or of being harmed. One could raise questions about the negative behaviors youths learn in jails and detention centers. Community policing, strong neighborhood crime watches, and partnerships among key institutions are credited with success.[18]

End Notes

What we learned is that the two interventions are effective, but costly. We did not see a concerted push that addressed both structural problems, especially the lack of legitimate work and work preparation and other mobilization of community and social services including individual, family, and group work and therapy. Clients overwhelmed by structural societal deficits and personal need will continue to require justice-based services and opportunity structures and decent work or expectation of work[19] early enough in their life cycle to prevent their joining up with a gang. For too many, the gang appears to be a long-standing solution to their problems. The existence of gangs speaks to the deficits in a nation that fails to direct its resources to better serve its more vulnerable citizens. A pivotal deficit is the lack of strong and successful public education.

In the 1950s social workers were often engaged in innovative work with gangs, forging greater understanding of the specialized theory and practice skills that are necessary to guide work with this population. The decline of the street worker and of settlement houses over the past two or more decades and the current lack of interest in work with the poor has meant that few professionally trained in social work or experienced in group activities are found on urban streets.

Finally, information on the gang problem is urgently needed by practitioners who will be called upon more and more to help overwhelmed families and to provide alternative systems and structures for societal and community support to gang members who are troubled and who have at best minimal constructive, mainstream resources at their disposal.

8

SOME LESSONS AND CONSIDERATIONS ABOUT GROUP INTERVENTIONS

INTRODUCTION

We began this work in efforts to determine why groups were not more widely used in clinical practice with overwhelmed clients since this intervention offered a strong opportunity for client growth and change. We wanted to explore the resistance to groups, but we especially wanted to find out what group leaders, both professional and nonprofessional, can bring to the various stages of group development and process. In this chapter, we factor out some lessons related to understanding context and population, starting up, processes and techniques that help move group members to stronger functioning, and the salience of values. We also discuss the resistance to groups per se and reasons why groups seem to have lower status than one-on-one forms of intervention. We have already discussed a conceptual framework that should prove helpful to practitioners, offering guideposts for facilitating change and predicting outcomes.

Having commented on all of the areas above, we now highlight some salient issues.

Understanding Context in Work with Overwhelmed Clients

Contextualization of clients' problems has gained acceptance among practitioners in the last decade. Understanding the person in his or her environment is now considered essential because many of the problems which overwhelmed clients bring are related to external stressors such as unemployment, income deficiency, poor education, and depleted neighborhoods which offer inadequate city services and spawn drug infestation. And all of these stressors are compounded by many forms of racism. Many of the bureaucrats that serve clients appear indifferent and uncaring in their dealings with people who do not present well (dress poorly, speak nonfluently). Clients often lack the socialization opportunities available to the middle-class at the same time that many of the bureaucrats who run the programs which overwhelmed clients use are middle class. The dissonance between the two can thwart positive interaction. Thus traditional psychological and physiological aspects of behavior are not the only areas targeted for examination and change with this population; environmental factors are also areas in which change must be sought.

Consistent with this perspective agencies and practitioners must focus more on community building and rebuilding initiatives. One thrust of these initiatives is to connect poor and overwhelmed people through community organizations to the norms, values, and resources of the wider community. We believe that agencies must play a strong role in bringing back bridge-building organizations that connect this population with the community. And yet there is slim evidence that this critical strategy for empowering this population is taking place.[1] What community mobilization and organization there has been is centered around gang suppression, with neighbors, police, and churches working together to address the gang problem. Agencies have done little to develop systemic organizational procedures for dealing with this population's problems, such as finding or developing jobs, job training, and education. Our sense is that clients who needed medical treatment were able to obtain it. The story was different, however, regarding decent and safe housing, good education, and employment opportunities.

Agencies must allocate funds not just to individual, family, and group clinical interventions as has been seen, but also for community building, organization, and development. We do not call on clinicians to do all of this work, but suggest that agencies employ community organizers and social planners who can help mobilize community change.

STRATEGIES AND TECHNIQUES THAT HELPED CLIENTS GROW AND CHANGE

Our examination of group intervention with several different groups revealed a number of strategies and techniques used to achieve both group and personal goals and to obtain successful outcomes. Process strategies such as teaching trust, encouraging risk taking, truth saying, and facing reality all proved beneficial in the groups. Similarly, practitioners drew from a repertoire of tools in working with the overwhelmed including the use of self-disclosure, role playing and rehearsing, modeling, mirroring, literature, art and music, story telling, externalization, metaphors, letter writing, and more. Several are identified and explored here in an effort to help both beginning and experienced practitioners learn from the contributions of those practicing with the overwhelmed population. Although practitioners differed in professional orientation and personal style, and worked for agencies with different philosophical views about service and service delivery, they were all skillful, knowledgeable, and effective in helping groups and individual members set goals and reach successful outcomes. Those practitioners worked to create the necessary supportive or therapeutic environment that encouraged growth and change.

Trust, Risk Taking, and Individual Change Within the Group

In order to grow and change, risk taking becomes central for all group members. Practitioners accept responsibility for creating a safe environment in which to take appropriate risks. For group members to move from a safe, well-defended old zone, whether desirable or not, requires taking a chance, in the face of an uncertain outcome. The need to change produces anxiety, fear, tension, and even anger in some overwhelmed clients. Members are vulnerable to many of the debilitating forces that brought them into the group in the first place—feeling abandoned, isolated, suffering loss, abusing others, and so on. The early contract that members agree to (to accept and buy into goals) helps them face up to this need for change to deal with that which is blocking improved functioning. It also extracts a commitment that they will strive to achieve that change in the context of the group which can at times be supportive, confrontational, and demanding.

Once in the group, individuals take risks because they seek approval of the other members as well as that of the practitioner. Healthy competition can provide the pressure that some need for movement. What happens is that pressure in the group helps create dissonance in a member's level of self-satisfaction. As a member deals with internal conflict, which can become heightened due to interaction with other members, he or she can begin to see what behaviors need to be worked on.[2]

We note that pressure for change does not emanate only from personal desire but rather from external forces which constitute systems of control in the lives of the overwhelmed. For example, before a client can have visitation rights restored or secure the return of a child the department of social services often mandates certain behavioral expectations. Such pressures can serve to counteract the momentum and depth of resistance to change.

The trust that is built within a group strengthens: as one member opens up, it is easier for a second and then others to do so. When a co-member takes risks and receives feedback—or perhaps fails to take enough risk—group members might then encourage more risks, including self-revealing behavior. Kottler discusses the place of the "risky shift" as a way of explaining why group decisions are bolder than individual ones. Whether because "responsibility is more diffuse, because riskiness is a cultural value, or because adventurous group norms force compliance, there is much evidence to suggest that group settings are ideal for promoting risk-taking behaviors."[3] Certainly in the gang, peer pressure helped push individuals into bolder behavior; in fact, boldness was required during initiation. Comparable behavior can be seen in other groups, for example, in the Well Children in HIV/AIDS Affected Families and both the Mothers' and Fathers' Recovering Addicts

Parenting groups. In this whole process the issue of trust is paramount. The initial risk taker will assume that role only if the leader has established an atmosphere of safety through modeling such risk taking herself. The leader must also convey the idea that risk-taking behavior promotes growth is expected. This enhances the perception that the group is safe, and the resulting sense of trust increases as members begin to view risk taking as positive and as growth producing.

Risk taking hardly takes place in early group sessions since members may feel intimidated by the presence of unfamiliar persons as well as the unfamiliar environment. We note that in all of the groups time was taken for initial introductions, icebreaking, and activities to help members feel relaxed. In the University Women of African Descent group the four corners art activity was used to help members feel comfortable as well as to help them structure their thoughts regarding concerns about college life. Once beyond the early sessions, different levels of risk taking became possible.

While the practitioner tries to create an environment that facilitates reasonable risk taking that is free of put-downs, badgering, and harsh coercion, there are nonetheless debilitating forces. These include fears and anxieties of members that they will not be able to change old behaviors (such as controlling the impulse to hit a companion or child) or that they will be unable to learn new ones (how to request and negotiate), that one will be rejected even though one worked to change behaviors (the DSS worker will not give back my child no matter what I do). There may be fear of disapproval (what will others think about my actions toward my family, my drugging past, my present struggle to stay away from drugs or drug money), anxieties about trying out new thinking (if I steal the bike I can get into serious trouble so I will think before I steal it), anxieties about being pushed or even feeling coerced (you have to understand other people's culture and get along in order to be successful), and great fear of expressing real feelings (removing the mask) because this means being vulnerable.

Practitioners help members navigate an uncharted course by first encouraging reasonable risks and self-disclosure, and then moving to feedback and to confrontation.[4] An example of the latter occurred in the Parenting Group for Recovering Addict Fathers when members assumed that the unemployed Hugo was lying about treating his wife to dinner and flowers. The practitioner permitted this confrontation, keeping the challenge in check and not allowing ridicule, abusive language, or swearing. She then directed the discussion so that members could understand how to improve relationships with their significant others and how to secure cooperation rather than opposition. Some of the techniques used to help members begin to take risks and start opening up are summarized below.

Self-Disclosure

As implied in the discussion on trust and risk taking, self-disclosure is an important tool. Offering herself as an example, the practitioner not only enhances members' sense of safety but shows "how to" when she shares appropriate personal information about herself. In using this technique, as well as others, practitioners must be aware that it is important to separate the self and one's own personal troubles from one's professional role. Practitioners must also be very careful to keep disclosure of personal coping strategies from slipping into bragging or modelling behavior that is unrealistic for clients.

Truth Saying

Practitioners helped members understand that they could grow and change by confronting difficulties in their lives and in their environment through teaching truth saying as a coping mechanism. This required members to be honest in sharing facts and information about their circumstances, to develop the ability to look at their actual reality, not dreams and fantasy, and move away from exaggeration and lying. This was a challenge for members who had developed various ways of avoiding the truth and adapting to the pain and discomfort that automatically had been so much a part of their circumstances.

In the University Women of African Descent group, there was discussion about "seeking after truth" to understand the historical reasons blacks used lying as a survival strategy and the need for them to face their reality honestly no matter how painful that might be. Similarly, in the Well Children in HIV/AIDS Affected Families group, practitioners held youths accountable for responsible truth saying. They encouraged them to face the personal fear, anger, denial, and agony embodied in their dreadful circumstances, including the extended, painful illness and likely death of a parent. The therapeutic goal of truthfulness was seen in the Vietnamese women's group when one member courageously revealed a long-held secret about her children's out-of-wedlock births.

Cognitive Restructuring

In helping members learn to change destructive thought patterns that keep them unable to function effectively, the leader enables them to identify self-devaluing thoughts and distorted cognitions related to other people and experiences, and encourages more appropriate thinking. Thinking through possible actions and predictable responses from individuals and institutions offered members options for new ways of operating by moving away from impulsive behavior. In the Well Children in HIV/AIDS Affected Families group we saw how the practitioner assisted the young members to examine their thinking before engaging in behavior that would be destructive.

Role Playing and Rehearsing

The technique of role playing was used in several groups, and very poignantly in some instances. The goal is to have group members revision themselves effectively handling a problematic issue and communication problem. As a member practices this approach, other members and the practitioner give feedback that the member uses as he repeats the role play and improves his performance. In the Parenting Group for Recovering Addict Fathers a member learned how to find a new way of addressing and speaking with a former companion who he felt blocked his parental visitation rights. For some members, however, role playing is inappropriate and may exaggerate discomfort and block motivations to change.

During the role play the practitioner serves as a coach, and cannot afford to show impatience or boredom no matter how hard a member is struggling. Neither can the practitioner allow one member to monopolize the role play as an attention-seeking maneuver. The practitioner must also be particularly alert to reactions from members who may become bored with the repeated episodes of role playing and the follow-up rehearsals. She must also be on watch for nonverbal behavior such as negative facial and body language that might send the role player a negative signal, causing withdrawal and thereby thwarting the opening-up process that is the intended result. On the other hand, feedback from members that is positive, clear, instructive, and embracing of the role player is what practitioners hope for. Role playing followed up with rehearsing is time consuming and emotionally demanding, but it offers members a good opportunity to improve their performance.

Modeling

Everything the practitioner does offers opportunity for clients to learn new ways of being and behaving. This is one reason why it is important that she present in a professional manner: in dress, in speech, in promptness within follow-up appointments, and in communicating correct information. Earlier we commented that the practitioner often constitutes the only contact clients have with middle-class persons who expect so much from the overwhelmed and who may hold many of the keys to their future.

Mirroring

Mirroring occurs when the practitioner acts out or imitates an action, behavior, or mannerism of a group member so that support and feedback can enable that member to correct ineffective, destructive, and inappropriate behavior. Mirroring was used by one of the practitioners in the University Women of African Descent group to demonstrate how the student's behavior could be viewed as off-putting to a professor.

Using Literature, Art, Music

Literature can be used as a tool for facilitating members' capacity to relate to painful issues. Characters and particular circumstances in stories that are similar to those of group members can give members a way to identify without feeling overly threatened. They are encouraged to also analyze and think through alternative paths, again mapping out what a character might have done. In the University Women of African Decent group literature was used to mobilize group process, allowing members to reach a comfort level more quickly and begin taking risk early on.

Similar advantages can be gained from the use of an art or music activity. A drawing of her family, encouraged by a co-leader, helped a member of the University Women of African Descent group to free herself of the shame she had internalized relative to not having had a father but rather, in her words, a "sperm donor." In several group examples music, including rap in the Well Children in HIV/AIDS Affected Families group, also became an important tool.

Story Telling

Here, the goal is to have group members tell their own stories in a way that is comfortable for them. Group leaders can structure story telling by asking for specific content: for example, how families celebrate national and religious holidays, family events such as birthdays, and joyous events such as a birth or a graduation from high school or college. As members learn to open up and disclose their personal stories often expand, and they demonstrate greater interest and engagement as story tellers. Members learn from these stories that others carry similar burdens and manage to cope, as they also learn from each other's coping experiences. Recall how Ms. A. in the Women Saving Face group of older Vietnamese women told her story, revealing her long-held secret of bearing a child fathered by an older man. Later, they had three other children, creating a family without having a legal marriage.

In the Well Children in HIV/AIDS Affected Families group the children were encouraged to tell their stories in order to share their pain, anger, sense of betrayal, and fear about "the family secret." The group process also showed the surprising resilience of the children and their capacity for finding joy in humor and creativity.

Externalization

Externalization is a strategy that allows group members to confront problem behavior as though it is outside of the self. Figures, symbols, and metaphors are used, for example, to represent out-of-control impulses and behaviors, which are then used as objects about which group members can speak. In the Well Children in HIV/AIDS Affected Families group, Mr. Monster was the character who represented the negatives in the lives of the children, with whom they were helped to dialogue, and express their feelings of anger, anxiety, and fear and devise strategies for control.

Undermining Labeling

Practitioners were always mindful to help clients set realistic goals and rules. Working with poor clients, they exerted care not to carry stereotypes in their minds or act on them through using pathological labels without attention to context. Such attention required them to focus also on interaction in context rather than merely on diagnosis as a way of understanding clients.

Processing: In the Present and for the Future

Practitioners encouraged members to think through their current circumstance (thinking in the present) and at the same time to consider future personal goals and status. While this was part of the process in all of the groups, The Women Moving Forward group and both of the recovering adult parenting groups placed a good deal of emphasis on this type of self-evaluation. Thinking about the future and a better life was especially hard in the therapeutic group for gang youth because so many did not envision themselves living beyond their early twenties, since death and loss were both prominent in their experiences.

Use of Metaphors

Metaphors can be used to help explain difficult or troublesome concepts and processes. Members can often relate more easily to a colorful, nonthreatening story than to a specific direction or suggestion. In the therapeutic group for gang youth the practitioner spoke clearly and often through use of metaphors and was able to interpret new expectations to these clients. In the Well Children in HIV/AIDS Affected Families group, Mr. Monster and sports metaphors were used to help members externalize problem behaviors. Mr. Monster, the children were told, was the cause of the miserable things happening to good people. They were encouraged to direct their feelings to him, talk to him, or yell at him so they could get him out of their psychological space and move on with their lives.

Letter Writing

Using this tool, group members can express the pain, anger, or frustration that they harbor toward other persons. It can be an effective outlet even though the target of the feelings is not present.

The Well Children in HIV/AIDS group members wrote to both living and deceased family members sharing their thoughts and pain. The members of the University Women of African Descent group wrote to themselves, outlining goals they wished to achieve, and recording their progress after sessions. One good aspect about letter writing is that letters do not have to be mailed nor must they become a part of any interactive dialogue.

Participation in Planning

Helping members participate in planning the activities of the group offered them an opportunity for experiencing a sense of control and mastery. This activity was used in nearly all of the groups.

Time Out

In the children's groups, time out was used when their behavior was characterized by lack of control as demonstrated by outbursts and other destructive acts. This technique requires the child to step out of the group for quiet down time. Sometimes, it was necessary to actively but respectfully assist the child to make this move out of the group temporarily. At times practitioners even carried those children out of the group who became very aggressive both verbally and physically.

Checking In

This practice allows members to express how they have progressed (or regressed) since the last meeting. Offering this opportunity at the beginning of each session helped reinforce the sense that the group was still a safe place for sharing feelings and attitudes. Most of the women's groups did this, and it consumed little time. In the University Women of African Descent group, for example, members said their hellos, and then talked about their week, recounting both good and sad events. Hearing from Mr. Right, not hearing from him, from parents, and others were sources of news to share, as well as success on an exam or a positive outcome after meeting with a professor.

Being Attentive

Practitioners must listen to individual group members and to the group process itself. A sure way to lose a group and to lose individuals is to be perceived as being inattentive. Practitioners listen and try to "get into" their clients' experiences. They must demonstrate that they are receptive to receiving all kinds of factual data which are then pulled together as a body of information about the group members and about the group.

What must be remembered is that many of the overwhelmed do not have supportive families, neighbors, and other resources. Thus the practitioner is likely to become a very important figure in the life of the group member.

Managing Anger

Practitioners often identified clients who were so consumed with anger and rage that they unknowingly blocked opportunities for better relationships. These clients could not see how anger tripped them up, yielding negative consequences. For example, the practitioners in the Well Children in HIV/AIDS Affected Families group offered instruction to the children on how to manage their anger and aggressive acting out. Often one practitioner would put his arms around the child whose anger was out of control and simply hold him—firmly but warmly. Sometimes, the child would have to be taken out of the group. There were also several examples of anger management with adult group members.

Identifying Game Playing And Redirecting Behaviors

Many overwhelmed clients have learned how to be successful in manipulating individuals, family members, friends, and even organizations. Clients are often quite intelligent and well aware of how to string clever stories in hope of achieving a short-term goal. The young woman who tried to join the University Women of African Descent group and use it as a bully pulpit against another woman with whom she had become embroiled in argument is an example. That she saw the group as a forum for her own agenda and an opportunity for manipulating others toward her position and against another student became obvious to the practitioners who interviewed her and who then declined to offer membership, referring her instead to another service for conflict mediation.

Manipulative behaviors were used by several of the men with whom women group members had relationships. The women learned to identify these behaviors, confront some, and ultimately to move on despite the pain that some of these actions produced. In the Recovering Addict Mothers' Parenting group, for example, one member identified her brother's unwillingness to shoulder any of the burdens of their household. She was eventually able to take the difficult step of putting him out, even though it meant that he would in effect be homeless. Her intent was not to hurt her brother but rather to protect her few resources so that she and her son could live a better life.

Communication: Explicit and Straightforward

Throughout the case presentations one can observe the value of explicit, straightforward commentary on the part of the practitioner in discussions with group members. Neither vague nor mystifying, these practitioners made their points using clear, concise statements. In work with gang youth, recall that the practitioner made a point of being very, very clear. To repeat, the practitioner made it clear, for example, that guns should not be brought into the group.

Another example is drawn from the Well Children in HIV/AIDS Affected Families group. Note how the practitioner was quite clear when he helped young Wayne to identify the "triggers" that would engulf him when he experienced the urge to steal. What practitioners must remember is that an individual's future is at stake and that clear communication can ensure safety and protection of both life and limb. Explicitness requires additional time, and the repeating and rehearsing of points as necessary.

SPIRITUALITY

It is imperative that practitioners working with the overwhelmed recognize the spiritual needs of clients. Many individuals may feel that they have few earthly supports. They believe that a greater power will help them through each day and they turn to a personal God for such assistance and guidance.

It has often been acknowledged that in homes of the African-American poor are three valued items: the Holy Bible, a picture of Martin Luther King, Jr., and one of the Kennedy brothers, John and Robert. It is also acknowledged that many poor people get down on their knees and pray.

In the groups presented here, spiritual needs did not surface directly, with the exception of one group, the Recovering Addict Fathers' Parenting group. What is important to note in that group process was that the practitioner did not cut off one member's repeated pleas that the men bring God into their lives but rather allowed him to present his view.

As more Americans feel a personal void in their lives, many are seeking a spiritual awakening. Thus, more clients and practitioners will undoubtedly feel freer to express spiritual conviction. Certainly in social work, new spirituality groups and sessions are being organized in the schools of social work. A new special interest association on spirituality is holding national sessions. In a short time, the profession can expect contributions to its literature on how to include this important but neglected subject in programs, curricula, or projects.

THE SALIENCE OF VALUES IN WORK WITH
OVERWHELMED CLIENTS

In all of this work it can be observed that practitioners introduced group members to certain values, ensuring that these values were understood and implemented throughout the group process.

Democratic Participation

One highly emphasized value was that of respect for democratic rules and governance. Some members were not accustomed to such an orientation. Familiar as they were with dominance/subordination and authoritarianism in relationships, they found democratic process a new experience. This was evident in the Women Moving Forward group, the Recovering Addict Mothers' Parenting group, and the Recovering Addict Fathers' Parenting group, which all demonstrated the authoritarian nature of the behavior of some of the men and how both men and women were introduced to and learned negotiation skills. Democratic participation was also new for those members who tended toward passivity or subordination in their interaction, having to be encouraged and coaxed into participation in the group. This was demonstrated in the initial sessions in the Vietnamese Women Saving Face group.

Acceptable Behavior

Establishing a set of values is critical in dealing with any group but can be particularly challenging, especially with gang-prone youth. Leaders must articulate values that promote nonviolence and rules that require acceptable behavior. Swearing, disrespectful communication, physical conflict, fighting, antisocial behavior, use of weapons, and aggressive acting out were not tolerated in the groups discussed here. In the Well Children of HIV/AIDS Affected Families group, the co-leaders removed children from the group when they engaged in aggressive, acting-out behavior, offering them time to calm down and chill out.

Respecting the Worth and Dignity of All Clients

Respecting the dignity of every individual was another much emphasized value. Gang members, aged widows, and young children all could sense that agencies cared for them as individuals and respected their human worth. Workers held all to high expectations, making no exceptions even when certain behavior among certain groups may have been culturally driven. For example, dominant male behavior as manifested in tolerance for battering women and striking children was not condoned.

Confidentiality and Privacy

Confidentiality and privacy are values that must be carefully upheld in the group. Members must be assisted to become accustomed to being open inside the group. At the same time, members' private troubles must be kept within the group's boundaries, never bridging the value of confidentiality. Members learned that loose talk back in the neighborhood about events that occurred in a group might place a vulnerable member in serious jeopardy. For example, visitation with children might be denied if certain information was incorrectly processed and presented to certain regulatory agency staff. There was special caution on this subject in both the mothers' and the fathers' parenting groups.

Safety

Safety was always a high priority to ensure that problematic circumstances would be shared. All knew that they shared responsibility for the safety of each other. Violent behavior was not acceptable behavior in any group. In the gang group bringing knives, guns, or drugs onto the premises was strictly prohibited. In the men's and mixed gender groups there was a clear understanding and acceptance of this stance from the beginning. The same was true of the women's groups.

THEORETICAL BASE FOR GROUP INTERVENTION

Theories (or Approaches) in Use Undergirding Group Practice

The approaches used by the practitioner in the therapeutic group drew heavily on empowerment theory, family systems theory, cognitive-behavioral theory, and social learning theory. Most of the groups presented were oriented to the use of strategies emphasizing support and education while the predominant theory in this work was empowerment. The central strategies of empowerment theory are building on personal strengths, helping clients to understand the entrapping nature of their own realities (contextualization), and education focused on the delivery of appropriate information regarding community and external resources along with knowledge of self.[5] In the Women Saving Face group, practitioners drew heavily on empowerment within a relational model of group dynamics which paid attention to members' connection to one another and sharing of one another's mutuality and empathy. Empowerment theory was buttressed with several other theories or

TABLE 8–1

Theories/Approaches Undergirding Groups

Group	Type of Group	Theory	Supplemental Theory/Approach
Women Moving Forward	Support	Empowerment Problem Solving	Communication
Parenting Group for Recovering Addict Mothers	Support	Empowerment	Communication Problem Solving
Parenting Group for Recovering Addict Fathers	Support	Empowerment	Communication Problem Solving
Women Saving Face	Support	Empowerment	Communication Problem Solving
University Women of African Descent	Support	Empowerment	Communication Social Learning Problem Solving
Well Children in HIV/AIDS Families	Support Education	Cognitive-Behavioral Family Systems Empowerment	Communication Social Learning Problem Solving
Gang Therapeutic Group	Therapeutic	Empowerment Family Systems Cognitive-Behavioral	Communication Social Learning Problem Solving
Mixed Gender Groups Privilege Parenting Education/ Growth	Therapeutic Support	Psychodynamic Empowerment	Communication Problem Solving

approaches including cognitive-behavioral, family systems, communication, social learning, education, and psychodynamic. See Table 8–1.

Cognitive-behavioral theory explains how people's thoughts and thinking processes maintain problem behaviors. Intervention based on this theory focuses on altering negative thinking and distorted beliefs and substituting constructive positive thinking, thereby producing new, more effective behaviors. Thus, in this approach, the practitioner's focus was on changing behavior through altering the group member's thinking process. The use of cognitive-behavioral approaches was evident in the Well Children in HIV/AIDS Families group where the techniques of role playing and restructuring helped Wayne to identify the thoughts and feelings that would trigger his motivation to steal. He was then helped to identify thoughts that would help block acting on this motivation, eventually substituting more constructive thoughts and behaviors.

Family systems theory describes and explains the roles and interactions among family members as individuals, in coalitions, and in interaction with other systems. Family systems theory was a focus in the therapeutic group for gang youth. A system is composed of many interactive components. Similarly, the family is composed of individuals who interact with one another, which means that they are dependent upon and interdependent with one another. As a system, the family relates to external systems. Thus, exchanges take place within the family system (among and between individuals and subsystems, i.e., parents and children). Exchanges also take place within the larger community (among and between family members and courts, police, schools, and welfare agencies). Well-adjusted and functioning family systems are able to change and adapt, meeting needs of members, helping individuals as interdependent parts to grow, receive necessary emotional nuturance, and function within appropriate limits. Much of the discussion on gang-prone youth showed that practitioners tried to learn as much as they could about a youth's family situation and also to work with the family system.

Social learning theory explains behavior as a result of identification and interaction. Interaction approaches relying on this theory emphasize modeling (by the practitioner) and identification (with the practitioner) by the client. Social learning theory was evident in many of the groups, serving as the basis for the widely used technique of modeling, and also, less often of mirroring. Although modeling was operative to some degree in all of the groups, we call attention to the University Women of African Descent group where one practitioner deliberately used her past experience with problems similar to those facing the students to demonstrate that a positive outcome could be possible. The same practitioner used mirroring in a few instances.

Communication theory was the basis for the activity and evaluation used in every group. Practitioners went to some effort to ensure that all members became aware that what they say must be clear and well understood by the listener and what they heard was what the speaker intended. They were coached to make statements to achieve the best receptivity. Miscommunication and distortion in messages are thus prevented.

In all of the groups practitioners used educational and problem-solving approaches. By giving group members relevant facts, information, and data, these processes assist members in developing effective ways for managing or dealing with problems that arise in life. This approach was most readily evident in the Well Children in HIV/AIDS Affected Families group, the University Women of African Descent group, and the Women Moving Forward group.

CONCERTED NEED FOR GROUP PROCESS IN
SOCIAL WORK CURRICULUM

Finally, the advantage of groups for this population is their multipurpose utility: they can be used for a variety of purposes and can be implemented in a variety of settings—schools, churches, private homes, social clubs/organizations, and the paid workplace. Employment settings have moved to offer more social services and groups since the 1970s, following the dramatic rise in numbers of women who now work. Given the need for groups and the successful interventions examined here, we return to the question raised earlier concerning the profession's resistance to groups.

In our contacts with agencies, we could find no programs where there was actual opposition to the use of group intervention. Most practitioners understand the value of groups. Their reluctance to use them is connected more to a professional affinity for individualized one-on-one clinical work than to actual negative attitudes about groups. There are, however, questions about widespread proficiency in work with groups. For example, the group work specialty area is one of the smallest in membership among social work specialties. The Council on Social Work Education which sets educational policy through the Commission on Accreditation has stipulated that all BSW and

MSW social work programs make content on groups mandatory;[6] however, the depth and breadth of such content is left to a school's discretion. Thus, coverage is uneven in the New England area and probably also across the country. The curriculum policy does not mandate a course or courses on groups but rather, course content. Since the mandate is nebulous, some programs offer only minimum content, for example, two sessions in a foundation practice course; other schools offer a basic course on social work with groups that examines group process; still others may offer a course on group therapy, perhaps along with a group process course. But even one or a few courses is barely adequate. The point is that at the present time the profession cannot count on having a large and robust cache of well-educated group workers.

ACCESS TO GROUPS FOR THE FUTURE

Managed Care and Work with the Overwhelmed

We acknowledge that there is increasing interest in group intervention. One reason is that more practitioners understand that group intervention is efficacious and can in fact be the intervention of choice with certain populations. Another reason for this growing interest is that groups can be cost-effective, permitting larger numbers of clients to be served by fewer practitioners. In one managed care agency it has been reported that the ratio of group therapy offerings in its service programs doubled in a six-month period, reaching 40 to 50 percent after the administrative team designed an implementation model. Outcome evaluation revealed that clients reported satisfaction while staff productivity obviously pleased management.[7] However this work and the results obtained were not conducted with the overwhelmed population.

Although there is, as yet, little hard evidence that clients fare less well under managed care than fee for service, the question remains as to how the use of groups can be made effective in a managed care environment where capitation (funding that is negotiated per capita for total care) presupposes services to be limited, practical, and of good quality. When so many needs must be met beyond the confines of the traditional therapeutic hour and even beyond the scope of the agency, ways must be found to implement the important direct work and advocacy work that practitioners now must perform in the new managed care setting. Similarly, community-building efforts must also be credited and financed. What will happen to the overwhelmed if in-person screening and initial interviews are replaced by telephone screenings? Will these clients become even more isolated, farther cut off from the mainstream? One potential benefit for the overwhelmed under managed care is that through better tracking and client management, they may have access to services that were not available from some agencies in the past. But these changes may reduce the self-determination of clients substantially with regard to selection of practitioners and treatment modalities. Practitioners likewise have many more constraints on their professional judgment and decision making.

Electronic Communication and Computer Networks

Electronic communication is also redefining access to groups for many. HIV/AIDS victims, for example, are often isolated not only because of the disease but also because poverty forces them to reside in deprived environments. Now, however, they can be involved in supportive non-face-to-face group experiences through daily telephone conferences. The role of the practitioner, however, is somewhat different: Missing are the direct human contact and all the cues and vibes that are significant for assessing progress and/or regression.

Computer networks offer new and expanded opportunity to establish virtual groups, communities, and organizations.

> These created entities support a broad range of human activities, including those related to employment and mutual aid. Vulnerable and overwhelmed clients can connect to sources of social support (with on-line self-help groups and self-care information) and employment opportunities via tele-community—the ability to do work at home and e-mail it into work if they can get assess to technology and the networks.[8]

As more cities make public access terminals available in libraries, community networks, and free nets, barriers that overwhelmed clients now face in gaining access to these new resources will be greatly reduced. Certainly, some groups will have the strengths to make use of this opportunity.

In an earlier book, *The Power to Care*, we lamented that some Americans have brought individualism to the level of ideology and suggested that, in common with all *-isms*, it has perhaps "entrapped us with some false gods," causing us to sacrifice individuals and communities.[9] We propose here that groups offer an opportunity for individuals to break out of their isolation and individualistic modes and move to positive dealings with common problems, issues, and personal pain with others by sharing the journey.[10]

NOTES

Chapter 1. A Mandate for Groups

1. J. G. Hopps, E. B. Pinderhughes, & R. Shankar (1995), *The Power to Care*, New York: Free Press.

Chapter 2. A Conceptual Framework for Group Intervention with Overwhelmed Clients

1. D. McClelland (1975), *Power: The Inner Experience*, New York: Wiley; and E. Pinderhughes (1995), "Empowering Diverse Populations: Family Practice Imperative for the 21st Century," *Families in Society*, 76(3)131–139.
2. D. Wrong (1980), *Power: Its Form, Base and Uses*, New York: Harper & Row, p. 3.
3. E. B. Pinderhughes (1995), "Empowering Diverse Populations: Family Practice Imperative for the 21st Century," *Families in Society*, 76(3)131-139; E. B. Pinderhughes (1989), *Understanding Race, Ethnicity and Power: Key to Efficacy in Clinical Practice*, New York: Free Press; see also M. Bowen (1978), *Family Therapy in Clinical Practice*, New York: Jason Aronson.
4. K. Chau (1991), "Social Work with Ethnic Minorities: Practice Issues and Potentials," *Journal of Multicultural Social Work* 1(1), 29–39.
5. H. Aponte (1994), *Bread and Spirit: Therapy with the New Poor*, New York: W.W. Norton.
6. E. B. Pinderhughes (1994), "Diversity and Populations at Risk: Ethnic Minorities and People of Color," in F.G. Reamer (Ed.), *The Foundations of Social Work Knowledge*, New York: Columbia Press; Pinderhughes (1989); and E. B. Pinderhughes (1973), "Racism in Psychotherapy," in C. Willie, B. Brown, & B. Karma (Eds.), *Racism and Mental Health*, Pittsburgh: University of Pittsburgh Press.
7. Pinderhughes (1973).
8. K. Reid (1995), *Social Work Practice with Groups: A Clinical Perspective*, Pacific Grove, CA: Brooks/Cole Publishing.

9. Ibid., p. 170.

10. B. Davidson and P. Jenkins (1989), "Class Diversity In Shelter Life," *Social Work,* 34(6) 491–495.

11. Reid (1995), p. 169.

12. B. McGowan (1988), "Helping Puerto Rican Families at Risk: Responsive Use of Time, Space and Relationships," in C. Jacobs and D. D. Bowles (Eds.), *Ethnicity and Race: Critical Concepts in Social Work,* Silver Spring, MD: National Association of Social Workers, pp. 48–70.

13. McGowan, (1988), p. 25

14. Ibid.

15. E. Imber-Black (1990), "Multiple Embedded Systems" in M. Mirkin (Ed.), *The Social And Political Contexts Of Family Therapy,* New York, NY: Allyn & Bacon, 3–18.

16. Pinderhughes (1989); and D. Heller (1985), *Power in Psychotherapeutic Practice,* New York: Human Services Press.

17. Ibid., p. 161.

18. D. Saleebey (1992), *The Strengths Perspective in Social Work Practice,* New York: Longman; and L. Gutierrez (1990), "Working with Women of Color: An Empowerment Perspective," *Social Work* 35: 149–153.

19. J. G. Hopps, E. B. Pinderhughes, and R. Shankar (1995), *The Power to Care: Clinical Practice Effectiveness with Overwhelmed Clients,* New York: Free Press, p. 135.

20. Ibid.

21. W. Grier and P. Cobbs (1968), *Black Rage,* New York: Basic Books.

22. E. B. Pinderhughes (1998), "Black Geneology Revisted: Restorying an African American Family," in M. M. Goldrick (Ed.), *Re-visioning Family Therapy: Race, Culture, and Gender in Clinical Practice,* New York: Guilford Press, 179–199.

Chapter 3. Group Formation and Development

1. B. Solomon (1976), *Black Empowerment,* New York: Columbia University Press; E. B. Pinderhughes (1983), "Empowerment for Our Clients and for Ourselves," *Social Case Work,* 64: 331–338.

2. J. A. Scholpler and M. J. Galinsky (1995), "Group Practice Overview," *Encyclopedia of Social Work,* 19th ed., p. 1129.

3. C. Garvin (1987), *Contemporary Group Work,* Englewood Cliffs, NJ: Prentice Hall, p. 92.

4. Scholpler and Galinsky (1995), p. 1135; Garvin (1987), pp. 95–96.

5. Garvin (1987), pp. 91–94; C. Zastrow (1993), *Social Work with Groups,* Chicago: Nelson-Hall Publishers, pp. 54–60.

6. Garvin (1987), pp. 80–148; J. Garland, H. Jones, and R. Kolodny (1965), "A Model for Stages and Development in Social Work Groups," in Bernstein, S. (Ed.), *Exploration in Group Work,* Boston: Boston University School of Social Work; L. Seliller (1995), "Stages of Development in Women's Groups: A Political Model," *Boston University School of Social Work Alumni Journal,* 6–7; E. Lewis (1992), "Regaining Promise: Feminist Perspectives for Social Group Work Practice," *Social Work with*

Groups 15(2–3): 271–284; I. Yalom (1985), *The Theory and Practice of Group Psychotherapy,* New York: Basic Books.

7. R. Toseland and R. Rivas (1995), *An Introduction to Group Work Practice,* Boston: Allyn & Bacon, p. 95.

8. Ibid., p. 98.

9. K. Chau (1991), "Social Work with Ethnic Minorities: Practice Issues and Potentials," *Journal of Multicultural Social Work* 1(1): 29–39; D. E. Hurdle (1990), "The Ethnic Group Experience," *Social Work with Groups,* 13(4): 59–69; L. Davis and E. Proctor (1989), *Race, Gender and Class: Guidelines for Practice with Individuals, Families and Groups,* Englewood Cliffs: Prentice-Hall, pp. 314–339; J. G. Hopps, E. B. Pinderhughes, and R. Shankar (1995), *The Power to Care: Clinical Practice Effectiveness with Overwhelmed Clients,* New York: Free Press; K. Chau (1992), *Needs Assessment for Group Work with People of Color: A Conceptual Formulation,* Haworth Press, Binghamton, NY, pp. 53–66; C. Garvin and B. Reed (1994), "Small Group Therapy and Social Work Practice: Promoting Diversity and Social Justice or Re-Creating Equities," in R. R. Greene (Ed.), *Human Behavior Theory: A Diversity Framework,* New York: Aldine De Gruyter.

10. E. B. Pinderhughes (1989), *Understanding Race, Ethnicity and Power,* New York: Free Press.

11. See Toseland and Rivas (1995) for discussion on "Autocratic, Democratic and Laissez-Faire Leader Behavior," p. 95.

12. Pinderhughes (1989).

13. Hopps, Pinderhughes, and Shankar (1995), pp. 53–55.

Note: The authors acknowledge contributions from the late Dr. Velma Hoover on practice with the overwhelmed population.

Chapter 4. Group Formation and Development

1. H. Aponte (1994). *Bread and Spirit: Therapy with the New Poor.* New York: W. W. Norton.

2. Ibid.; E. B. Pinderhughes (1989), *Understanding Race, Ethnicity and Power,* New York: Free Press.

3. K. E. Reid (1997), *Social Work Practice with Groups.* 2nd ed., Pacific Grove, CA: Brooks/Cole. pp. 45–46.

4. J. G. Hopps, E. B. Pinderhughes, and R. Shankar (1995), *The Power to Care: Clinical Practice Effectiveness with Overwhelmed Clients,* New York: Free Press.

Chapter 5. Women's and Children's Groups

1. T. V. Tran (1988), "The Vietnamese American Family," in C. H. Mindel, B. W. Havernstein, and R. Wright, (Eds.), *Ethnic Families in America, Patterns and Variations,* New York, Amsterdam, London: Elsevier.

2. Ibid.; T. V. Tran R. Wright, and C. H. Mindel (1987), "Alienation Among Viet-

namese Refugees in the United States: A Causal Approach," *Journal of Social Service Research* 11(1): 59–75.

3. Tran (1987, 1988).

4. S. S. DeHooper and T. V. Tran (1987), "Social Work with Asian Americans," *Journal of Independent Social Work* 1(4): 51–62; D. Lynn (1997), *Smoking Cessation in Older Vietnamese Americans*, Ann Arbor, MI: UMI Dissertation Services.

5. R. Kurkland and R. Salmon (1995), *Group Work Practice in a Troubled Society: Problems and Opportunities*, New York: Haworth Press; J. A. Scholpler & M. J. Galinsky (1995), *Social Group Work Competence: Our Strengths and Challenges*, 33–43.

6. Tran (1987, 1988).

7. A. O. Freed (1988), "Interviewing Through an Interpreter," *Social Work* 33(4): 315–319.

8. Ibid., p. 315.

9. DeHooper and Tran (1987).

10. M. Schwartz-Thomsen and D. Lynn (1996), private communication to Hopps and Pinderhughes.

11. R. Mollica and Y. Caspi-Yavin (1991), "Measuring Torture and Torture-Related Symptons," *Psychological Assessment* 3(4): 581–587.

12. Schwartz-Thomsen and Lynn (1996).

13. Ibid.

14. Freed (1988).

15. Ibid.

16. Lynn (1997).

17. b. hooks (1993), *Sisters of the Yam: Black Women and Self-Recovery*, Boston: South End Press.

18. T. McMillan (1987), *Mama*, Boston: Houghton-Mifflin.

19. D. West (1909/1995) *The Wedding—1st Edition*, New York: Doubleday.

20. K. Reid (1991), *Social Work Practice with Groups: A Clinical Perspective*, Pacific Grove, CA: Brooks/Cole Publishing, pp. 112–113, 126–127, 182, 210.

21. J. H. Scholpler and M. J. Galinsky (1995), "Group Practice Overview," *Encyclopedia of Social Work, 19th Edition*, NASW Press, Wash. D. C. pp. 1129–42.

22. hooks (1993), p. 13.

23. Ibid.

24. Ibid.

25. Ibid., p. 22; see also Pinderhughes (1996).

26. hooks (1993), p. 26.

27. W. E. Sedlacek (1988), "Black Students on White Campuses: 20 Years of Research," *Journal of College-Student Personnel* 28(6): 484–495.

28. J. R. Feagin (1992), "The Continuing Significance of Racism: Discrimination Against Black Students in White Colleges," *The Journal of Black Studies* 22(4): 546–578.

29. D. E. Mack, T. W. Tucker, et al. (1997), "Interethnic Relations on Campus: Can't We All Get Along?" *Journal of Multicultural Counseling and Development* 25: 256–268.

30. hooks (1993), p. 32.

31. hooks (1993), p. 33; also see Pinderhughes, *The Power to Care* (1989, 1995), for dis-

cussion of this behavior as a response to oppression and entrapment in a powerless role, which aims to convey a sense of power.

32. hooks (1993), p. 33.

33. Ibid.

34. L. Davis (1996), "Different Effects of Racial Composition on Male and Female Groups: Implications for Group Work Practice," *Social Work Research* 20(3): 157–66; Davis, Chen & Strew.

35. See Hopps, Pinderhughes and Shankar (1995), *The Power to Care*, 101–102, for an example of how to use a social work intervention strategy to help a teenage client cope with racism.

36. Reid (1991), p. 112.

37. Ibid., p. 120.

38. J. R. Feagin and M. P. Sikes (1995), "How Black Students Cope with Racism on White Campuses," *Journal of Blacks in Higher Education* 8: 91–97.

39. Feagin (1992), pp. 91–97.

40. H. Kamya (1997), "Groupwork with Children from HIV/AIDS Affected Families" *Journal of HIV/AIDS Prevention & Education for Adolescents & Children* 1(2): 74. Hawthorne Press, Inc. and Michaels & Levine (1992), 268:3456–3461—"Estimates of the Number of Motherless Youth Orphaned by AIDS in the United States," *Journal of the American Medical Association.*

41. J. Vastola, A. Nierenberg, and E. K. Graham (1994), "The Lost and Found Group: Work with Bereaved Children," in A. Gitterman and L. Shulman, (Eds.), *Mutual Aid Groups, Vulnerable Populations and the Life Cycles,* New York: Columbia University Press, pp. 81–96.

42. Kamya (1997), p. 75.

43. Hopps, Pinderhughes, and Shankar (1995).

44. Pinderhughes (1996).

45. Hopps, Pinderhughes, Shankar (1995).

46. H. Kamya (in press), *Group Techniques with Children Living in HIV/AIDS Affected Families*

Chapter 6. Mixed Groups

1. T. Walsh (1997), unpublished paper, Boston College Graduate School of Social Work.

2. J. G. Hopps, E. B. Pinderhughes, and R. Shankar (1995), *The Power to Care,* New York: Free Press.

3. L. Davis and E. Proctor (1989), *Race, Gender and Class,* Englewood Cliffs: Prentice Hall.

4. Hopps, Pinderhughes, and Shankar (1995).

5. Ibid.

6. H. I. Kaplan and B. J. Sadock (1998), *Synopsis of Psychiatry: Behavioral Sciences Clinical Psychiatry,* Baltimore: Williams & Wilkins, p. 405. Kaplan and Sadock stated that ". . . a recent survey conducted by the National Institute on Drug Abuse found that over 15% of the U.S. population older than 18 years have serious substance

use problems, two-thirds of which are primarily alcohol related. Another study conducted by the Substance Abuse and Mental Health Research Administration found that 111,000,000 persons ages 12 and over had used alcohol in the past month which translates into 52% of the population. About 32,000,000 people engaged in binge drinking and 11,000,000 were heavy drinkers" (p. 378).

"In 1995 whites continued to have the highest rate of alcohol use at 56%. Rates for Hispanics and blacks were 45% and 41%, respectively. The rate of binge use was lower among blacks (11.2%) than whites (16.6%) and Hispanics (17.2%). Heavy use showed no statistically significant differences of race or ethnicity (5.7% for whites, 6.3% for Hispanics and 4.6% for blacks)" (p. 392).

"Sixty percent of men were past month alcohol users compared with 45% of women. Men were more likely than women to be binge drinkers (23.8% and 8.5%, respectively). And heavy drinkers (9.4% and 2.0%), respectively" (p. 392).

7. Davis and Proctor (1989).

Chapter 7. The Gang Groups

1. D. Balk (1995), *Adolescent Development: Early Through Late Adolescents,* Pacific Grove, CA: Brooks/Cole Publishers. Balk reviewed gang studies and developed three theoretical classifications as cited by Branch (1997). See also C. W. Branch (1997), *Clinical Interventions with Gang Adolescents and Their Families,* Boulder, Colorado: Westview Press; F. Clark (1996), *Teenage Street Gangs: Differences, Membership and Intervention.* Sacramento, California; *Op. Cit* Monti, D. (1993), *Op. Cit* Pinderhughes, H., *Op. Cit* R. D. Putnam (1995), "Bowling Alone: America's Declining Social Capital," *Journal of Democracy* 6(1): 65–78; C. Taylor (1990), *Dangerous Society.* East Lansing, MI: University Press.

2. Ibid. Branch (1997); M. Pinderhughes, Ibid., (1995).

3. C. Taylor, *Op. Cit*

4. In some instances names have been adopted from professional sports teams. Thus, for example, the Brown (street) Bears would name themselves after the Chicago Bears professional football team, or the King (street) Bulls (after the Chicago Bulls professional basketball team. Colors are also used as forms of identification. Some local gangs are affiliated with the "Crips" (blue) or the "Bloods" (red), gangs that started in Los Angeles and are now nationwide.

5. One account of the history of the Crips relates how the gang began as a social group with distinguishing dress that included left handed gloves, an earring on the left ear, a blue railroad handkerchief, and a cane. Later the Avenue, a group from the east side of Los Angeles, became the new Crips, the name coming from their gait which was a limping swaggering walk—thus "Crips," short for crippled. After the devastating mid-sixties Watts riots, African-Americans greeted one another, "Hey Blood" in an attempt to promote racial solidarity, and a red handkerchief became their symbol. See Clark (1996).

6. C. Huff (1993), "Gangs in the United States," In A.P. Goldstein and C. Huff (Eds.), *The Gang Intervention Handbook,* Champaign, IL: Research.

7. The unlawful assembly is common law supported by case laws, state laws, and municipal ordinances; see: 71 A.L.R. Digest 2d 875; Unlawful assembly (1995) Lawyers Cooperative Publishing Company

8. H. Aponte (1994) *Bread and Spirit: Therapy with the New Poor*, New York: W.W. Norton.

9. Taylor (1990) *Op. Cit*; Clark (1996) *Op. Cit*. pg. 3;

10. Personal communications to authors; and see Cummings and Monti (1993).

11. D. J. Monti (1993) "Origins and Problems of Gang Research in the United States" in S. Cummings and D. J. Monti. (Eds.) *Gangs*.

12. K. Hardy, at Syracuse University provided data for discussion in personal communication with E. B. Pinderhughes.

13. Hardy & Laszloffy (In Press)

14. Branch (1997). *Op. Cit*.

15. Aponte (1994). *Op. Cit*.

16. K. Cullen (1996; Jan. 7), "The Neighborhood Cop," *The Boston Globe Magazine*; A. Martin (Apr. 13), "Gangs May Be Too Diverse for Single Remedy," *The Chicago Tribune*, Sec. 4C.

17. A. Chise (August 29, 1997), "Crime Rate at 29 Year Low in the City," *The Boston Globe*.

18. Ibid.

19. J. G. Hopps, E. B. Pinderhughes, and R. Shankar (1995), *The Power to Care*, New York: Free Press.

Chapter 8. Some Lessons and Considerations About Group Interventions

1. J. G. Hopps, E. B. Pinderhughes, and R. Shankar (1995), *The Power to Care*, New York: Free Press.

2. J. Kottler (1994), *Advanced Group Leadership*, Pacific Grove, CA: Books-Cole Publishing.

3. Ibid. p. 211.

4. Ibid.

5. E. B. Pinderhughes (1989), *Understanding Race, Ethnicity and Power: Keys to Efficacy in Clincial Practice*, New York: Free Press.

6. Council on Social Work Education and Curriculum Policy Statement (1992). Arlington, Virginia.

7. N. Winegan, J. Bistline, and S. Sheridan (1992), "Implementing a Group Therapy Program in a Managed-Care Setting: Combining Cost Effectiveness and Quality Care," *Families In Society: The Journal of Contemporary Human Services*

8. J. McNutt (1998), unpublished paper, Boston College.

9. Hopps, Pinderhughes, and Shankar (1995).

10. R. Wuthnow (1994), *Sharing the Journey: Support Groups and America's New Quest for Community*, New York: Free Press.

INDEX

agency: philosophy of, 67–68; responsibility of, 45

agenda building in groups, 49–54

AIDS. *See* Well Children in HIV/AIDS Affected Families Group

alcohol-sobriety groups, 126–132; goals and rules, 126; group composition, 127–128; process, 128–132; purpose and formation, 126. *See also* Parenting Group for Recovering Addict Fathers; Parenting Group for Recovering Addict Mothers

anger, managing, 181

art, using in groups, 177–178

attentive, being, in groups, 181

behavior: clarifying expectations in, 44–45; cognitive, 19, 176, 186; coping, 10–15; fighting as response in, 28; game playing and redirecting, 181–182; manipulative, 182; powerlessness and power in, 8–19; reactive, 11, 14–15; survival, 17–21

checking in, in groups, 180–181

children: involvement of parents through, 29; vulnerability of, 2–3. *See also* Well Children in HIV/AIDS Affected Families Group; women and children's groups

class status, impact of, on power, 10–15

clients: strategies and techniques that helped, to grow and change, 172–183. *See also* overwhelmed clients

clinical effectiveness, 1

cognitive-behavioral approaches in managing survival behaviors, 19

cognitive-behavioral theory, 186

cognitive restructuring in groups, 176

commercial gang, 144

communication: electronic, 190–191; in groups, 182; pace of, and need for translation, 98–99; rules for clear, 163; structure, 45–46

communication theory, 187–188

confidentiality, in groups, 73–74, 184–185

confrontation, 162–163

contextualization of clients' problems, 171

coping behaviors to lack of power, 10–15

corporate gang, 144

co-therapists in group facilitation, 123–124

Council on Social Work Education in setting of educational policy, 188–189

democratic participation, 183–184

distrust, norm of, 37–38

drug addiction. *See* Parenting Group for Recovering Addict Fathers; Parenting Group for Recovering Addict Mothers

Printed in the United States
58278LVS00006B/325-342

9 780743 237864